cool containers

cool
containers

Adam Caplin

photography by Marianne Majerus

jacqui
small

First published in 2003 by Jacqui Small
an imprint of Aurum Press Ltd
25 Bedford Avenue
London WC1B 3AT

Text © Adam Caplin 2003
Photography © Marianne Majerus 2003
Layout and design © Jacqui Small 2003

Publisher **Jacqui Small**
Editor **Bella Pringle**
Designers **Maggie Town, Beverly Price**
Production **Geoff Barlow**

British Library Cataloguing-in-Publication
data: A catalogue record for this book is
available from the British Library.

ISBN 1 903 221 15 3

Every effort has been made to ensure that
all the information in this book is accurate.
However, due to differing conditions and
individual skills, the Publisher cannot be
responsible for any injuries, losses, and
other damages which may result from the
use of the information in this book.

Printed in Hong Kong.

2005 2004 2003
10 9 8 7 6 5 4 3 2 1

contents

why containers?

Ever since I first started gardening, at the tender age of five, I was always fascinated by plant pots. Small terracotta pots that fitted into old horticultural wooden boxes were like a puzzle (a very easy one) and large plastic pots helped me imagine that I had superhuman strength as I carried three above my head.

My father was a gardener who was ahead of his time, and used plants in pots to help change the look of the garden over a weekend, moving cacti from the greenhouse in the early summer and bedding out his own-grown plants into an eclectic mix of containers. They tended to be small displays, filled with a few of the traditional bedding plants – lobelia, alyssum and geraniums. Our garden soil was alkaline so we grew acid-loving plants like camellias in large containers so that they could sit happily in their preferred soil mix.

Once I had my own garden and gardening career, trips overseas helped to broaden my mind. Not only was the food delicious in Italy, but the plants looked majestic in their old terracotta "homes". Large oranges and lemons spoke of impossible dreams, gnarled olive trees and oleanders seemed a distant fantasy. While on a smaller scale, old olive tins, plastic barrels and metal containers were planted with bougainvillea, jasmine and fragrant basil.

People started to bring ideas back, and container gardening became far more creative as gardeners began to take the containers, and the freedom and opportunities that they bring really seriously. The fusion of all sorts of influences means that it is no longer a surprise to see a fruiting lemon in

▶ Contemporary gardens are ideal places for containers, particularly if there are no flower beds or borders. These galvanised metal boxes fit in perfectly with the other hard landscaping materials and provide plenty of space for substantial plants like bamboos.

the most unlikely city location, or "exotics" like oleanders and bird-of-paradise on a terrace half way up a skyscraper. Moving these less hardy plants indoors during winter and outside again in summer is just one of the practicalities that we are becoming familiar with. Containers have helped the gardener to become more versatile with his or her planting and has expanded our plant vocabulary. Species that were unknown or difficult to grow outside all year round have now entered the gardening language.

As homes and gardens have become smaller, people have become more interested in making the most of any available space, so container gardens have grown in popularity. For a roof garden or balcony, where there is no soil for planting, containers make gardening possible. These gardens often occupy difficult sites from tiny roof spaces surrounded by buildings that cast a shadow, to narrow balconies and small dark basement areas – places that may have been ignored before. Containers are a blessing for those of us with such a limited landscape.

Moving house or apartment more frequently has also encouraged people to regard plants grown in containers as possessions, to be taken with them to their new home. And now plants that were once considered invasive when grown in the open flower bed, like bamboos, can be planted up in pots and will thrive in the confined space when their root-growth is restricted.

◀ Traditional flower borders can be given structure and atmosphere with the introduction of well-placed planted containers. Here, magnificent agaves in terracotta pots give focus to a large colourful border, as well as an increased sense of perspective and a classical edge.

▶ In small courtyard gardens, containers become incredibly valuable. Here a shallow bowl is planted up with small succulents and grasses to create a garden in miniature.

Planted containers are particularly valuable in contemporary gardens that are trying to establish one coherent theme. The containers act as extensions of the planting space and can add tremendous impact by using more daring plantings like palms and small trees. The availability of container materials, like more refined concretes and galvanised metals at affordable prices, plus larger sizes and better designs, have increased the range of containers on the market, and made it easier to integrate the container with any style of garden. This needn't always be modern, as many people like to use container plantings to recreate the atmosphere of other cultures. I still enjoy bringing the flavour of Italy into the garden by using traditional terracotta.

Planted containers are more than just a garden accessory. They can be joyful and uplifting, full of spring cheer and hope, they can glow like the summer sun and they can banish the winter blues. I love the magic of plants, combine that with the creativity of the pot maker, and you can become a garden artist when putting the two together.

This book is intended as a guide to what is possible, to help you open your mind to the potential of planted containers in your own garden space. The planting ideas will show you how to get the most out of your containers and your plants. Whether you live out of town or on the twentieth floor of an apartment block, let your planted containers help make gardening more fun, and your garden more rewarding at all times of the year.

◀ Areas that have more extreme conditions like this windy balcony are common because of high-rise living. Lack of space means that even the smallest area cannot be overlooked. Pines in buckets help to bring nature in to this most urban of settings.

▶ A dark basement garden can be transformed into a cool, relaxing area by using well chosen plants in large containers. I particularly like the use of bold plants, like this dwarf fan palm (*Chamaerops humilis*) and arum lily (*Zantedeschia aethiopica*) which contrast with the delicate cut leaf of an acer.

design

the setting

By choosing the most appropriate container for your outside space, in terms of the container style and choice of material, you can improve the look of your existing site and garden setting as well as making a strong display.

Containers come in so many diverse styles and materials that I still find when confronted with a good pot display that I feel a little like a child in a sweet shop. It is easy to get carried away when around every corner is temptation; a lovely terracotta long tomato pot, a terrazzo square pot or a concrete bowl, all competing for my attention. But it is important to remember

that when too many different styles of containers are placed en masse in the garden the whole scene can appear a bit muddled. Better to be selective – buying the wrong containers can be an expensive mistake.

Taking the style of your house and garden into consideration will help you decide on the types of container that will look most appropriate. The backbone of

◀ The geometric patterns of this outdoor space, with its straight lines, is the perfect setting for this row of square pots. The straight stems of the black bamboo topped by soft foliage provides a link between the hard surfaces and nature beyond the garden.

▼ The "lollipop" topiary flanking the doorway mirror the box balls at the base of the steps making a smooth transition between house and garden.

many contemporary gardens is powerful hard landscaping, and the garden walls and paths often appear to be an extension of the house, enclosing the outdoor area so that it feels like an "outside room". These gardens are ruled by the desire to achieve sharp lines and clarity, and so the planting schemes often rely on strong foliage shapes. Finding containers that fit in with this vision really helps to strengthen this effect. For example, a tall white concrete pot filled with the sharp leaves of a cordyline would look perfectly at home in a garden with white plastered walls, while square terracotta containers would be a good choice for a

modern garden design based on a square grid system. To create a coherent picture, choose containers in materials that are similar to the fabric of the garden structure, in colours that complement the dominant tones. The whole impact of the design relies on a degree of control – using heavy-duty materials like concrete or stone, clear-cut lines, containers in simple shapes and distinct foliage.

Very formal garden spaces are dominated by structure and the use of repeated motifs and they call for similarly systematic container plantings. Remember that the best container schemes enhance what is already there and do not challenge it. A formal

garden containing rows of clipped box hedges, or waves of lavender, asks for simple containers with similar formal-style plantings.

Informal gardens offer a less restrictive palette and fewer limitations than modern gardens. I love the sense of time, growth and decay, and the dominance of plants and flower borders. Here, the more traditional containers often look best, particularly the earthy colours of terracotta and wood, stone and wicker, which all feel like natural occurrences in the landscape. The choice of container plants can echo the garden planting and containers placed in borders appear as though they are growing out of the garden setting. Slight imperfections, often found with old terracotta and hand-thrown pots, are lovely and mirror the imperfections of nature.

Gardens created from an eclectic mix of plants and unusual objects and materials are better equipped to absorb many different styles of containers. My own personal favourites for a really creative wild garden are recycled containers, which look as though they were born for the purpose. My own little "urban beach" garden is strewn with cockle shells and has several old tea chests planted up with evergreens.

The main view from the house into the garden is often an important place for containers. My terrace is outside the living-room window and I have arranged my pots so that they can be seen from the inside to help integrate the indoor space with what is outside.

There are times and places where a bold container which offers a contrast to the surroundings may be appropriate. If there is an ugly view that you would like to play down, a really eye-catching container can help to divert the eye. A container that stands out from its background will be seen more clearly from the house, and can bring a forgotten area of the garden to life.

When you are looking back at the house from the garden or when containers are standing in an entrance, the house becomes the context in which the container is seen. An imposing frontage needs similarly chunky containers with real structural planting to balance its proportions. A simple, painted front door provides the opportunity for a cheery planting of tulips in a glazed container, or the enthusiastic welcome of marigolds in a hand-painted terracotta planter. I really like to show a little bit of the personality of the home owner when choosing containers for entrance sites. Plants in pots painted by children and their friends can offer a lovely

◀ A beautiful relaxed garden is a lovely setting for an overflow of colour and growth from a copper container. This display of verbena, argyranthemum and diascia is eye-catching and mixes well with the surrounding landscape.

▶ This sheltered urban garden is enclosed by bamboos and eucalyptus, while modern containers punctuate the space. The choice of terracotta blends well with the wall, and repetition gives rhythm to the space.

◀ Walls provide an excellent opportunity for a container planting. Here, one of the most evocative of plants – a fruiting lemon – is trained as a wall shrub and turns the space into a Mediterranean scene. Planting the lemon tree in a container makes it easy to move this tender plant indoors when the weather turns cold.

▶ A little half-pot attached to the wall can add colour and interest without taking up too much space or looking unbalanced.

▶▶ An old metal barrel sits in front of a vivid pink wall to create interest and perspective. The fruiting grape vine is a real treasure.

welcome. A modern frontage which is perhaps more stylised and minimal in appearance, calls for modern terracotta shapes, concrete, metal or fibreglass.

The front of the house is an area that you see throughout the year when you leave and arrive back home. It frustrates me to see flimsy containers full of half-dead bedding plants at entrances looking rather disappointed to see you leave, and equally disappointed when you arrive back. For a welcoming entrance, choose a large, heavy container (difficult to steal) and plant it with something like the evergreen *Pieris formosa* 'Wakehurst', which flowers in spring, or a camellia if the site is shady.

roof gardens and balconies

On a practical note, roof gardens and balconies often require lightweight containers, not only because of these structures' load-bearing restrictions, but also to make carrying the pots up any stairs, and out onto the roof, easier. The choice of container may be governed by the setting. In an area where a roof terrace is surrounded by older-style brick buildings, I've seen terracotta, old cast-iron baths and aged wood work well, while in an urban roof terrace setting surrounded by modern building structures of glass, steel and concrete, galvanised metal and fibreglass containers look great.

On a veranda, wood containers made from untreated hardwoods, or stained or painted softwoods can help to smooth the transition from the house to the garden.

Use materials for containers that mimic those of the veranda, while planting up the pots with plants that suit the garden aspect.

awkward areas

There are areas of the garden which tend to be more difficult to plant up, and require containers because there is no flower bed space. Walls next to houses or on the patio often suffer from this problem, and this is where container plantings can help. Though it is extraordinary what plants will endure, try to give the plant access to as much soil as possible to help it establish a healthy root system. If the site puts limits on the size of container, choose a deep one, because the greater the volume of soil the greater the plant's capacity for growth; also, deep soil will retain more water. If you cannot access the site easily, consider installing an automatic irrigation system to prevent plants in awkward areas from drying out.

Walls also provide the opportunity for growing plants in hanging containers. In narrow passages and small courtyard patios, they offer what is often the only available surface for gardening. Hanging containers and half-pots are also useful for growing plants in narrow sites which people have to negotiate in order to get out into the garden proper. Choose containers made from robust materials which are free of sharp edges to make them safe when you brush past along a passageway. Wood containers are suitable as are galvanised metal pots with rolled edges. Plastic and fibreglass are acceptable although they tend to be a bit lightweight and may get blown over.

scale

Finding the most appropriate size of container for the available space is important and will help create realistic planting opportunities, and improve the overall appearance of the garden.

It is tempting to fill up a small space with lots of small containers, particularly as it sounds logical that the more pots you have the larger the space feels. However, this can produce the very opposite effect, making a small area look desperately busy.

One of the most effective tiny gardens I've ever seen has a large-scale pot against the wall, planted with a beautiful weeping birch tree. The container appears disproportionately large for the space, taking up about 25 per cent of the floor space. However, this area which had previously been dominated by its imposing walls was transformed and the tree in its container became the focal point. The choice of tree was key, its weeping form providing a ceiling of branches that stopped the eye from travelling too high.

A large wall really does need to be balanced by a good-sized container. It will also provide more root space for a climber or tree and a more secure anchorage.

In any garden I try to buy the large-scale pots first, just like planting a permanent garden, where the framework plants – the trees, large shrubs and hedges – are the most important elements. Often it is the plant effect that matters most, a large plant may be required to provide screening and a focal point on a hard surface and the pot size has to fit with the scale of plant. A tree, large bamboo or palm will need a large container for cultural reasons, to provide stability and to create a balance between the plant and the container.

If the most important feature of the space is the view out of a window, then a container using small compact plants is ideal, particularly if you don't want to block that view. Often, a view simply needs underlining with plants.

An intimate space in a larger garden can look more cosy with smaller pots like *Primula auriculas* on a stand, alpines and herbs in a corner. Placing them near where people sit, or where people stop means that you can study the beauty of the flower.

A couple of larger containers at the end of the garden can enliven a view. One of my most substantial pots is nestled at the back tucked into a verdant corner. It can only just be seen from the terrace and helps create some mystery, making people curious and wanting to explore further.

On a practical note, if you are buying a large pot for the garden, think of access and weight. It is important to check that the new container can get into the garden and that the weight of a fully planted and watered container isn't dangerous if load-bearing is an issue.

▲ Small terracotta pots help to highlight and set off the beauty of an individual delicate flower like this *Primula auricula*.

◀ Using large containers and some substantial plants like phormiums, hostas and an acer helps reduce the impact of the wall and make a small space look bigger.

grouping and repetition

The grouping and repetition of planted containers can help to create an integrated scene that has dramatic impact and is harmonious, compared to the low-impact effect of dotting them around all over the terrace or garden.

Gardens have often relied on containers as focal points, a single urn in the centre of a circle, or a pair of urns announcing the transition from the hard landscaping of the terrace to the soft greens of borders and lawn. However, a group of carefully arranged containers can transform the garden creating a fuller, and more all-year-round effect where a single planter might look a little lost and ineffectual.

In a small space, particularly where the flower bed space is limited, a group of containers not only looks dramatic, but provides far more planting opportunities.

A wall against paving which would otherwise be bare can become a backdrop for containers and plants. Informal groupings of containers can work well, particularly if the background is monotonous, because the contrasting styles of containers can be really eye-catching and help to liven up a dull view.

In a really tiny space, restricting the style of containers is easier on the eye than an informal mixed grouping. As with all of these choices, it's really a matter of taste. Collectors, and people who can't help adding more and more things to the garden and house

◀ A group of similar bowl-shaped containers look natural when placed together in a group. Plant them up with succulents like sedums and sempervivums to highlight the harmony of the group and to help create a coherent display that is both interesting and comforting.

▶ A more eclectic mix of grasses, palms and pots provides a variety of interest and helps to draw attention away from the fencing. Grouping them together in a haphazard way makes the display seem more relaxed and informal.

probably get as much pleasure from the hunt for containers and plants as from planting them, and they are far more likely to have an eclectic mix, which can be charming and fits in with their personal style.

In a more contemporary garden the use of pot repetition helps perspective and harmony. A border interrupted by a series of identical tall containers feels like a mix of the classical and modern, with pedestals for plants surrounded by flowers and foliage. These displays can also make the garden appear longer or wider if arranged either along the length of a flower bed or if they are taken across the end of the space. Visual tricks can also be used. By placing two similar style containers one in the foreground and a smaller one in the distance you can use perspective to create the impression of a larger garden. Repetition will often involve putting containers in flower beds, and this is delightful and challenging because it looks as though the containers have become part of the planting.

Grouping similar containers together can be a comforting and beautiful feature. Similar plantings tend to fit well in a group like this. I avoid having too much colour in any one pot as I find that they can end up

looking too "corporate", which I dislike. The whole effect of a group of similar pots should be a harmony of foliage, flower shapes and materials.

Windowsills, balconies and roof gardens have a more practical need for grouping, because there is no flower bed space. Individual pots grouped together help to protect each other, particularly in a windy position. A wind-tolerant plant like a bamboo in a larger container can act as protection for smaller, more delicate plants. A compact basil in front of a larger terracotta pot gets enough protection in the summer to grow and crop well. The larger container also makes an attractive background colour for these smaller pots. Grouping also enables you to water more easily. I try to keep real moisture-lovers near each other and those that prefer dry conditions together as well.

Planted containers on windowsills should reflect the style of the house – a contemporary house requires complementary containers. The group will often benefit from repetition of simple pots and plants, as this fits in with the lines and symmetry of the house. Older houses often require a similar treatment so as not to disturb the frontage. I choose plants and containers in muted colours.

◀ Herbs grown in identical pots look very reassuring and wholesome. I love the way the different growing habits of the plants really show themselves off from the laid-back catmint in the foreground to the feathery fennel at the back.

▲ On a windowsill, where space is limited, using similar pots makes sense. Too much of a mix might appear chaotic, and planting them all with skimmia offers diversity without confusion.

Repetition can also be reassuring, offering a point of reference particularly if it is difficult to see where the boundary begins and ends. That is why using controllable and reliable evergreen like box and pittosporum, and the architecture of powerful evergreens like phormiums and bamboos can help to mark out your territory, especially on a roof terrace.

The more informal the garden, particularly if lots of different types of plants and materials are used, the more informal the grouping of containers can be. At its fullest my garden had at least three major groupings, one for edibles in mixed containers, another for shade-loving ferns and hostas in wood and the last for a few weird plants in recycled objects.

A group of containers on view from a living-room window can be a beautiful addition to the garden picture, and it is here that containers can be at their most flexible. I love to be able to change this picture once in a while, to make sure that these groups are always looking good. I grow some perennials in plastic containers, which are slipped into more permanent pots when they are budding, and then moved into a less prominent position when out of flower. One group of pots has an agapanthus for summer and autumn (the seedheads look splendid in autumn), skimmia for autumn and winter, a group of *Primula vulgaris* for early spring and hostas for spring and early summer.

▼ These clipped box shapes in large galvanised metal containers work well set against this panoramic cityscape. Their shape gives a sense of solidity and "grounding" to this high-rise garden.

◀ This display of hot colours with red cuphea, blue lobelia and purple phormium has a warmth to it and bursts out like a natural explosion of generosity from this wooden barrel. Flower and foliage colours can produce powerful emotional effects.

▶ I like the idea of being greeted by this cheerful flowering window box. The petunias and geraniums offer a stunning colour combination and produce huge quantities of flowers throughout the summer. Although the tonal range is modest this display appears incredibly opulent.

colour

Containers now come in a dazzling and bewildering range of colours offering the gardener more choice and potentially more confusion. How do you select the colours that are most suited to your garden space?

I remember my own excitement in the 1980s on first seeing the colourful new glazes on containers imported from the Far East. I planted a red-leafed Japanese maple in a brown dragon-pattern pot to recreate a little bit of the Orient in a shady corner of the garden, and white trumpet lilies in the dark blue glazed stoneware pot. The following year, glazed terracotta became fashionable, and the smart cream colours looked lovely planted with pale violas. By the time shiny galvanised metal window boxes made an appearance, my garden had started to look like a mixed collection of work in an art gallery – interesting when the containers were seen in isolation, but with no sense of unity.

Colourful containers, both machine- and handmade, which make use of the various stone and terracotta glazes, look wonderful planted up simply, and even better if they match something already planted in the garden. Pink glaze stoneware, for example, can look lovely near a pink flowering quince, while the greys and blacks of concrete and stone pots work well in a modern garden alongside dark purple cotinus.

In general, warm colours tend to be passionate and intense, while cooler colours are more relaxing. I love the bright, vibrant colours of the Mediterranean – old painted barrels full of bright begonias and bright plastic buckets – all framed by the sunlit glow of a whitewashed wall. The sheer exuberance of the scene is like a celebration of life. The temptation on coming home is to recreate this mood, filling up brightly coloured containers with shocking purples, intense blues and joyful yellows. The bright colours that expressed themselves so clearly against the blue sky and bright sun appear less vivid in northern temperate climates and sadly it is hard to recreate the same feeling.

In shade, use pale plant colours to help lighten the atmosphere. Pastel shades will look more natural than bright colours, as they reflect the little light that is available. Choose containers from a range of natural colours – pots that blend in with the background and do not stand out too much. Darker foliage and flower colours can be useful if you want to enhance the feeling of reflective melancholy in shady areas. Ferns and other dark, leafy foliage, like fatsia and *Viburnum davidii* are ideal, as are shade-loving flowers like periwinkles (*Vinca* species). Keep the container colour dark, or use old materials like stone and encourage the pots to grow moss and weather.

▼ A pyramid of red, orange and primrose-yellow *Ipomoea lobata*, and the fiery coral red flowers of *Fuchsia* 'Thalia'. These two look perfectly at home in front of a glorious display of climbing clematis.

▶ Individual concrete containers add a touch of artistry to the garden. This one is like an abstract painting with its purple base rising to its gold-green top of mind-your-own-business (*Helxine soleirolii*).

One advantage of container gardening is that you can use pots to add colour to the garden and they are portable. A predominantly green background might benefit from a pale yellow splash of nicotiana flowers, or the blue-grey leaves of *Hosta sieboldiana*. A sunny area can be transformed by introducing a blazing red-flowered salvia, or plants with soft grey and silver foliage, such as lavenders, *Convolvulus cneorum* or the simple cut-leaved cineraria. The neutral tones offered by silver and grey foliage will fit in with most container material including galvanised metal or bleached wood.

I think that limiting the colour palette for your choice of container and plants is worthwhile as there is a formidable range of tones in any single colour. Blue-flowered plants range from the startling intensity of *Ceanothus* 'Puget Blue' through to the gorgeous pale blue of *Clematis* 'Perle d'Azur'. The deep reds of *Clematis* 'Ernest Markham' contrast with the wonderful burgundy of *Pelargonium* 'Lord Bute'. Even white varies enormously – my favourite white shrub is *Exochorda* x *macrantha* 'The Bride'. More recently, new bedding plants have increased the available palette. I particularly like the range of mauve and blue verbenas, and the attractive and diverse half-hardy salvias and penstemons.

The most prominent colour in gardens is green, which comes in almost every shade. Use these differences when planting up your pots. Chamomile spilling over a terracotta rim in front of a darker green background of foliage is a comforting picture.

Solid blocks of colour grown in containers appear more substantial, particularly in contemporary garden settings. Here, I tend to mix fewer plants to achieve more striking results. Foliage colour is important. The black grass *Ophiopogon planiscapus* 'Nigrescens' is stunning in a container, as is the fabulous range of coleus leaf colours.

As the year advances the pattern of the sun changes. In my city garden, the terrace is in partial shade by midsummer as the branches of an overhanging tree come into full leaf, so I move containers with bright-coloured flowers to the sunniest position and also move those that need the sun to ripen their fruits, such as tomatoes and aubergines.

Favourite colours are as important in the garden as they are in the house and can be used to create harmony between indoors and out. I like to carry some of the interior colours outside as well as bringing some of the exterior inside. My indoor container is the smaller version of the one just outside the window and is painted in the same sandstone colour. The little citrus tree inside the living room helps to integrate the scene.

texture

Natural plant textures help to add character to the garden, creating interesting effects in all four seasons. Containers can complement these textures and act as a foil for flowers and foliage to show them off to best advantage.

Containers add many unique textures that would otherwise be missing in the garden, from the fine-grained look of terracotta to the hard reflective surface of zinc. Containers not only bring their own textures but also act as a foil for foliage and flowers, high-lighting, complementing and contrasting with different parts of the plant structure. For example, the soft foliage of woolly thyme (*Thymus pseudolanuginosus*) creeping over the rim of a stone or concrete pot makes for a fascinating contrast. Textures help to create real depth and feeling in the garden, and are an important and subtle addition to the gardener's palette.

The surfaces in a modern garden are usually quite prominent, relying on reflective panels and hard paths, walls and platforms to create an effect. Containers can either contrast with or complement these surfaces. The starkness of a new concrete container can stand proud and strong against a rendered wall, reinforcing its solidity.

The slightly rougher look of some materials can be used to great effect, particularly the grainier surface of weathered stone, concrete and terracotta. I think that it is the mix of container and plant textures that helps to create a lovely garden, and it is by experimenting with these effects that you will introduce an extra dimension.

▲ Geometric scale-like patterns on this pot create a texture which is accentuated by the spiky leaves of a sempervivum.

◀ Containers introduce important texture to the garden. This terracotta urn contrasts with the frothy flowers of gypsophila and shows off the structure of a trailing sedum.

ageing

Some containers look more distinguished with the passing of time. Use the natural processes of weathering and ageing to add character to your outdoor space.

The changing appearance of garden containers as they get older and are exposed to the elements helps to remind us that the garden is not an enclosed room but a living organic space, where it rains, gets cold, and once in a while, the sun shines!

An old weathered pot looks so full of horticultural wisdom and character. It is such a contrast to other areas of life, where signs of wear-and-tear like damp on a wall or rust on the car are so unwelcome.

Metal containers age in a variety of ways, and the contrast between brand-new metal and rust brings the most dramatic change in as little as six weeks. Copper

when it ages oxidises to a gorgeous green verdigris, which is one of the most wonderful of colours in the garden.

In my garden I love rusting metal, and as a painter I often try to reproduce its warm brown tones on canvas. Rust has an interesting texture, and can create a lovely background for the right plant, a purple-leaved phormium, the bronze of an acer and the dark tones of *Pittosporum* 'Tom Thumb'.

Some metals are treated so that they do not age too quickly, particularly those made of galvanised metal and stainless steel, while others are expected to oxidise and rust with time to produce a completely different effect from new.

Containers in those metals that remain untouched by the ageing process are well-suited to small modern gardens, where maintaining the glossy sheen of the material is important as they are expected to match

◀◀ An old food tin quickly ages to produce a textured rusty effect. The mottled purple leaves of heuchera are the ideal partner to create a harmonious and attractive display.

◀ The stems of black bamboo look stunning growing amongst the russet and brown tones of a weathered metal trough. Decay like this in the garden is a reminder of the beauty and power of nature.

the unchanging fabric of the house or urban landscape. Galvanised metal containers seen against the sleek metal and glass materials of modern buildings rely on this.

terracotta

Different types of terracotta age in different ways. Dark-coloured, heavy-weight, machine-manufactured terracotta tends to age with less grace than some of the hand-thrown pots due to an oil that is added to the clay during production to make it more malleable. The lighter colour of Vietnamese, Malaysian and Chinese pots ages very quickly. The hand-thrown, dark-coloured terracotta clays can age really beautifully, but often take longer than Asian pots to

achieve this effect. A well-aged pot is truly magnificent and most take about five years from new before they start to look their best.

Being impatient, I like to speed up the ageing process, and often buy old containers for their imperfections. You can encourage ageing, particularly algae and moss growth on terracotta, concrete and stone by smearing the surface with yoghurt or fresh horse manure. The best condition to encourage silvering is a sunny position. The slight silvering effect on terracotta is a result of the salts leaching out of the material.

ageing wood

Wood containers decay in different ways depending on the type of wood and where

the containers are situated. Like terracotta, wood will become silvered in the sun, which looks very attractive, giving a seaside sun-bleached effect. Damp and shady conditions will encourage untreated wood to rot. This can be a problem for large wooden containers because they may eventually fall apart and will also attract woodlice. To help prevent wood containers from rotting, scorch the interior surface with a flame gun to create an inert surface that won't rot.

concrete and stone

These materials have porous surfaces that absorb water which encourages the growth of moss and algae. To keep stone and concrete looking clean and modern, spray the surface with a transparent waterproofing sealant (available from aquatic centres) to stop the water from being absorbed.

◀◀ A mixture of containers provides plenty of opportunities to show off the different ageing processes, from the silvering of terracotta to the algae and moss growth on concrete. Moss creeping over pot surfaces can soften hard edges and creates a subtle background for plants.

◀ Herbs seem to be natural partners for really well-weathered containers. I think there is a special relationship between aromatic edibles and the earthiness of older pots.

▶ The gentle silvering of old wooden market boxes helps to create a seaside atmosphere on this roof terrace. Plants like the blue-grey grass (*Festuca glauca*), the sea holly (*Eryngium* species) and other grey leaves help to reinforce this image.

materials

terracotta

There are many different types, styles and shapes of terracotta. Selecting pots that are going to be most appropriate for your contemporary or traditional garden is key as are the plants and planting schemes that will help the containers look their best.

If there were only one material available to make plant containers, I would choose terracotta. It is rooted in horticultural tradition and some of the first-known containers for plants were made out of this natural material. One of the most beautiful and romantic gardens I have ever seen was an old derelict garden in Italy, where ancient terracotta containers stood proud but empty while everything else around them was gracefully falling apart.

As well as being extremely beautiful, terracotta provides a good home for the roots of plants. The material is naturally porous and so supplies oxygen to the roots and also ensures good drainage. It stays cool even in the heat of the summer sun.

Nowadays terracotta pots are easy to find as they are made in Italy, France, Great Britain, America, and increasingly in China and Vietnam. Each type has its own appeal and the clay from which they are made, the mix, the finish and the drying process all contribute to their character. Regional differences can be significant, and pots made by individual potters are distinct. Maybe that is what makes terracotta containers so marvellous – the slight nuances in colour, the way the material ages, the texture and shape that all help to define their character.

◀◀ This wonderful empty olive jar appears to have been planted in a border surrounded by fennel and other sun-loving plants. You can almost feel the heat in this Mediterranean scene.

◀ A lime-washed jar fits into the enclosed space of a basement garden. The daisy-like flowers of erigeron and white gaura intermingle to complete a light, subtle and natural display.

▲ Terracotta is extremely versatile and has an important place in the modern garden. This contemporary triangular shape filled with the striking sword-like foliage of a silver astelia sits confidently in front of a rusting steel panel.

The earthy colours of terracotta rarely look out of place in any style of garden. Large, light and good value square and rectangular planters (now mainly imported from the Far East) are ideal for the enclosed, often rectangular smaller space of many urban gardens, roof terraces and balconies. The traditional shapes are still lovely, and the "long tom" – so-called because it was once used to grow tomatoes – is a slender and exquisite pot that has timeless appeal. Formal gardens look elegant with topiary planted in large terracotta containers, more natural informal-style gardens with penstemons creeping over the edge of an aged pot, modern gardens with the architectural dark green leaves of fatsias in large circular

clay pots. I can hardly think of a plant that does not benefit from an association with terracotta.

The versatility of clay also means that containers can be moulded or hand-thrown in a variety of shapes. Hand-thrown terracotta containers are more individual, with slight variations in shape, and when placed together make a charming family group. Some of these pots, particularly from small, quality suppliers are very special with prices to match. These are well suited to plants that will grow for many years in the container. Plants like citrus, vines, olives and figs are a natural partner for these, majestically ageing together, which creates an incredible feeling of permanence.

Machined terracotta often has a much smoother, more regular finish and tends to be less expensive than hand-thrown pots. But even with machined pots it is still possible to find some variation, and I often actually prefer slightly irregular machined pots (as long as they have not cracked during the firing process) as these have a bit more character. However, if you are buying a group of pots to create a modern, symmetrical effect, machine-made pots are ideal, not only because they are great value, but you can be sure that they are identical.

Beautiful individual pieces often deserve a special place in the garden, and require less planting as attention should focus on the pot. I can never understand the desire to cover a beautiful pot with a shaggy mop of flowers when it is the container itself that is the subject. These are often classical in shape, an urn, an ali-baba or a more modern shape like a tall cylinder. Rhubarb forcers are one of those wonderful shapes that seem to look great whether planted up or not. They were used to help force rhubarb into growth early in the season. There are also sea-kale forcers which keep the early shoots of sea kale blanched. Pots such as these give the garden an atmosphere of tradition, expertise and earthiness, creating a happy association with the walled gardens of the past.

◀ Glazed terracotta pots have become a valuable addition to the garden. This green pot provides an attractive base for spring bulb displays, and its smooth surface shows no signs of ageing.

▶ This subtle grey glaze tinged with lilac introduces a modern colour palette to the garden. I like the calm and serene nature of this glaze, which works well with plants such as orange-petalled Icelandic poppies (*Papaver nudicaule*) and the large-leaved pineapple plant (*Eucomis* species).

◀ The finish of terracotta depends on the clay from which it is made. These pots are produced from a clay mined in one particular area in Zimbabwe, which gives it a unique, very grainy texture which works well with the spiky ornamental grasses.

▶ An updated version of the long tom shows how this classic and simple design has endured. This stylish sleek shape looks wonderful paired up with topiary shapes.

▼ A mature calamondin completely transforms the atmosphere of a border, introducing an exotic edge. Citrus trees are excellent partners for terracotta, not only looking good but appreciating the porous, free-draining nature of the material.

Glazed terracotta is rather beautiful, either completely glazed, or partially to allow some of the clay to show through. I like these partial glazes, as terracotta is such a lovely material it seems such a shame to cover the whole thing up.

If placing pots in gardens in cold regions, always check that the terracotta is frost-resistant. The containers that are most vulnerable to cracking in freezing conditions are those that have been air dried. This drying technique used to be more common with pots made in Vietnam, China and Spain, however, most are now dried in a kiln and are sold with a guarantee of frost-hardiness. Guard against poor drainage by adding plenty of crocks to the bottom of the pot before adding the soil and make sure that there are adequate drainage holes. Soil that becomes waterlogged in a container will expand as it freezes and this can cause the pot to crack.

Terracotta is quite a brittle material and may break if knocked over or if accidentally hit by a gardening tool or passing wheelbarrow. Try to avoid placing these containers in "heavy traffic areas" where there is the potential for this sort of damage. Pots that have a narrow base are also far less stable than square-sided ones, so avoid putting taller plants in these containers if your site is exposed or windy.

During the summer months, sitting the base of the container in a saucer of water is a good idea. Terracotta is a porous material that dries out quickly and a couple of weeks unwatered in the summer may kill off the plants. Before going away, move the containers into a shady site, and sit them on saucers with a thin layer of gravel to help the plant take up water more slowly.

Pot "feet" for large containers can look splendid, and they also help to improve root aeration and drainage. I would only consider them for large-scale pots, particularly as they can make smaller pots unstable, and I also think that pot feet are a bit too grand for the smaller containers.

METHOD

• Plant up when the danger of frost has passed.

• Place a layer of crocks in the bottom of the container to improve drainage and use a peat-free, multi-purpose compost.

• To encourage a continuous display of flowers, ensure that the plants are well-fed throughout the summer months with a liquid tomato food. Deadhead the geraniums regularly.

• Overwinter the geraniums in a light frost-free area. 'Lotusland' requires constant warmth through the winter and is best kept in a heated greenhouse. Keep the potting compost quite dry and cut back hard before putting out again in mid-spring in a frost-free site.

baked earth

This smooth, boulder-shaped terracotta basin creates a simple brownish-red base for a vibrant pink and red flower mix. The jagged-edged variegated leaves of the geranium hide the rim of the terracotta pot and help to blur the boundary between the pot and the plants. I appreciate the positive energy of this display – a bit like fireworks bursting out of the container – and the long flowering season of both geraniums and pinks makes this dazzling arrangement particularly rewarding.

PLANTING MATERIALS

Large terracotta container (machine-manufactured in the Far East)

Terracotta crocks

Peat-free multi-purpose compost

PLANTS

Geranium PELGARDINI 'Lotusland'

Geranium FIREWORKS 'Salmon'

Dianthus species with maroon-eyed pale pink flowers with deeply fringed petals

PLANT ALTERNATIVES

Geranium 'Occold Shield' (golden leaf)

Geranium 'Vancouver Centennial' (purple leaf)

Plectranthus 'Sasha' (golden foliage)

PLANTING MATERIALS

Heavy-duty terracotta window box

Crocks

Soil-based compost and peat-free multi-purpose compost

PLANTS

Nicotiana – green or white flowered cultivars

Impatiens species

Helichrysum petiolare

Linum perenne

METHOD

• Make sure that the window box has drainage holes.

• Add an equal mix of soil-based and peat-free multi-purpose compost. Soil-based compost adds weight and therefore stability to the container, and also holds nutrients for longer.

• Plant in spring after the danger of frost has passed. Keep the plants well-watered and fed with a flower food. (This container is densely planted so will be greedy for moisture.) It will flower all summer and into autumn.

• Trim back the trailing silver helichrysum leaves if they become too overgrown and dominant in the container.

• Deadhead the nicotiana flowers as they die back to help prolong their flowering period.

country-style terracotta

A window box when planted up should look full and voluptuous, creating the effect of a miniature overgrown garden in a limited space. Window boxes, particularly when making a seasonal summer splash, should be generous and welcoming. Here, the lime-green nicotiana flowers, white busy lizzies and vivid blue flax flowers create an informal-style planting that will brighten up an area that doesn't receive much direct sunlight. All these plants, including trailing helichrysum will thrive in the limited space of the container, spilling over the edges to form a full display that will last throughout the summer months and into autumn.

METHOD

• Drill drainage holes in the container base (*see Care section*) if none are present. Add several crocks and plant in an equal mix of peat-free multi-purpose compost and soil-based compost.

• Plant up this summer display in mid-spring when frost is unlikely to occur.

• Keep well fed with flower food. Deadhead the argyranthemum regularly to encourage the optimum number of flowers.

• Cut back lightly in autumn.

• Argyranthemums can be over-wintered in a cool, light, frost-free area such as greenhouse or conservatory.

• Prune hard and feed the following spring before planting out once again.

summer apricots

Here, the mix of palm-like leaves of cordyline, half-hardy argyranthemum daisies and seasonal material such as blue lobelia, orange mimulus and salmon-pink verbena combine well to make one arrangement. The volume of flowering material in this container produces a really spectacular display, and all these plants can survive without too much moisture so co-exist quite happily. The plant combination grows best when placed in a sunny site and will last throughout the summer. The cordyline leaves are the only permanent element and act as a framework for this splendid summer display. In autumn, replace the summer-flowering material with violas and pansies for winter interest.

PLANTING MATERIALS

Terracotta urn from Crete

Crocks

1 part soil-based compost to 1 part peat-free multi-purpose compost

PLANTS

Argyranthemum

Cordyline australis 'Purpurea'

Lobelia erinus

Mimulus aurantiacus

Verbena x *hybrida* 'Salmon'

PLANT ALTERNATIVES

Brachyscome

Cordyline australis 'Sundance'

Diascia

Osteospermum

In a contemporary garden, stone containers can appear like part of the hard landscaping, fitting in well with rendered concrete walls and raised beds. In a cottage garden, stone containers blend seamlessly with the natural world, providing planting space for saxifrage, and the many different types of sedums.

Solid stone containers, like old stone sinks and troughs originally used for feeding animals are extremely beautiful and really worth making a fuss of. Make the container an important feature in the garden, planting it up to help show off its beauty. In sunny sites, fill stone troughs with alpines and compact growers like sedums, the wonderful tiny-leafed raoulia which forms a very tight mat, or even some of the really slow-growing conifers. These solid stone containers are incredibly heavy to transport, and you'll need help when positioning them in your chosen site. Troughs made of reconstituted stone, or "hypertufa" – a concrete and peat mix – are lighter. They are good value though not a terribly convincing alternative to the real thing.

One of the more recent introductions are stone containers called terrazzo. These have a concrete core and are surrounded by chipped stones set in resin. They are less brittle than some of the reconstituted stone containers due to this resin content. The stone is polished to produce a fine reflective surface in colours ranging from pure white to dark grey. Terrazzo containers are cast in lots of shapes and offer good value.

Tall terrazzo cylinders look good in contemporary gardens, simply planted with the silver-grey of astelia foliage, or the black grassy blades of *Ophiopogon planiscapus* 'Nigrescens'. Use foliage or flowers to enhance the container colour but make sure that the container is not obscured by plant material.

Glazed stoneware comes in a wide range of colours and has become an important product for the modern gardener. I love some of their deep powerful blues, dark pinks and greys, which offer a strong framework.

◀ One of the new generation of terrazzo planters made from stone chippings set in resin has a fascinating surface similar to marble. Its simplicity is enhanced by pure white tulips.

▶ A pale grey stone bowl planted with grape hyacinths looks effective because the diminutive plants do not distract from the beauty of the bowl. A mulch of slate chippings helps to anchor the plants.

stone

Containers made from stone are magnificent, and are really worth giving a prominent place in the garden. They are heavy, solid and provide a wonderful feeling of permanence. In a world where everything seems so transient and manufactured, stone is a real treat.

These bright container colours will set the tone for the garden, so take care when choosing them. (I prefer to use stone containers that are easy to blend with the garden design and planting scheme. This is one of the strengths of neutral-coloured containers.) You need to be very sure of your design when using large stone glazed containers in strong colours. These striking pots are best used as a deliberate foil for plants. Place them in a flower bed as a stand-alone feature, or behind pots that have been planted up. Silvery foliage, like artemisia planted in front of a deep blue terrazzo pot is a lovely combination.

Reconstituted stone in urn shapes that mimic designs from the past are valuable for recreating historic garden designs. They are also useful for fusing old and new styles. I have seen modern gardens where classical-shaped reconstituted stone containers create an interesting contrast to modern features. The urns often look a little too new at first, but soon weather to resemble old stone.

◀ A wonderful old stone trough has a beautiful appearance which is worth showing off. A mix of succulents and trailing geraniums fills the interior of the trough without covering up the front facade.

▼ Slate can make wonderful and attractive containers that fit into most styles of garden. There is something very modern in both the colour and the simplicity of slate. I make my own slate containers by facing plastic planters with old slate roof tiles. I have also seen this done with thin pieces of York stone, though their weight and irregular shape make this difficult.

METHOD

• Drill drainage holes and fill up half the pot with the broken pieces of stone to act as drainage crocks.

• Use a lightweight filler such as broken up polystyrene trays, to half-fill the pot and prevent it from becoming too heavy to move to its intended location.

• Fill in between the pieces of polystyrene with peat-free multi-purpose compost.

• Early in the season, plant 3–5 young coleus plants. Coleus grows very quickly as summer bedding, so it will soon fill out this large pot. Trim back the stems regularly to encourage bushy growth.

• Feed with nitrogen-rich food in the summer and trim to keep the plants bushy.

• Keep the display well-watered and do not let it dry out.

pink glaze

This summer and autumn display is vibrantly simple, both in the choice of plants and dark pink glazed stoneware container which help to set off one another. Sometimes a single species planting just can't be bettered as this colourful display goes to show. Early in the season, before it is warm enough to plant out the coleus, you could grow bulbs like the early spring-flowering reticulata iris to create a succession of colour. You can overwinter the coleus plants by moving the container into a cool, light place such as a greenhouse or conservatory. Keep the plants relatively dry. However, they are quite temperamental and even when kept in these conditions the coleus may need replacing the following spring.

PLANTING MATERIALS

Glazed stoneware container 1m (3ft) tall

Crocks

Broken polystyrene or similar lightweight filler

Peat-free multi-purpose compost

PLANTS

Coleus 'Black Dragon' (dark red leaves)

PLANT ALTERNATIVES

Other *Coleus* species

Iresine herbstii

Melissa officinalis

PLANTING MATERIALS

Stone trough

Crocks

1 part soil-based compost to 1 part peat-free multi-purpose compost

PLANTS

Bidens ferulifolia

Petunia 'Purple Wave'

Petunia 'Surfinia'

Scaevola aemula

PLANT ALTERNATIVES

Euryops pectinatus

Felicia amelloides

Tropaeolum Jewel Series (Nasturtium)

Verbena 'Sissinghurst'

METHOD

• Drilling the base of a stone container to make drainage holes is hard work. You need a powerful, slow drill with a masonry bit. If this proves too difficult, use crushed charcoal and gravel for drainage, and plant the display in a plastic container inside the stone.

• Plant up the display in spring using an equal mix of peat-free multi-purpose compost and soil-based compost.

• Feed the display with a flower food and nip back straggly growth during the summer, deadheading when necessary.

• In mid- to late summer when the petunias start to look straggly, cut them back and feed them to encourage new growth and more flowers.

trailing petunia trough

Wonderful examples of stone planters such as this can be found in antique shops that specialise in garden ornaments. Beware of the weight though, it'll need at least two people to carry it! When choosing container plants, I like to buy them in flower so that I can play with the colours to make sure that they work in harmony with the stone. Trailing *Petunia* 'Surfinia' is a new type and a good choice as it produces an abundance of flowers over a long season, many of which are scented, and it is fairly weather-resistant (meaning that the petunia flower petals don't damage easily). The darker blue-purple petals and paler blue scaevola, work well against the stone while the yellow bidens enliven the top of the display without interrupting the front edge of the trough.

concrete

Plant containers manufactured from concrete have made a comeback, with different finishes and styles now available. Use concrete planters in your garden to help integrate plant material with the range of hard surfaces that surround us.

Concrete has undergone a revival. No longer limited in its association with the grey, drab surface of buildings constructed in the 1950s and '60s, concrete has a fresh and modern appeal.

Concrete containers can be cast into almost any shape, and now there is a great variety of surface finishes available including one that allows for a smooth polished finish the texture and colour of limestone. Advances in colour technology have begun to produce some inspiring new colour tones and effects in concrete.

Thin-walled concrete containers are available in large, square, rectangular or circular shapes, and are relatively lightweight. They are suitable for roof gardens and balconies where load-bearing might be an issue. To ensure that they are strong, the thin-walled concrete is usually reinforced with fibreglass. This also makes it less brittle. Thin-walled concrete containers look slightly "retro", and can contribute a Modernist feel. In the '60s thin-walled concrete planters were used in public spaces so I think that they have to be planted up really well to avoid associations with these municipal schemes.

Thicker-walled concrete containers belong to a newer generation of planters. They are easier to find and are better value than thin-walled concrete pots. They look good in small urban gardens where there is a high proportion of hard landscaping material to foliage, flowers and lawn. If the garden is surrounded by buildings, walls and hard surfaces, concrete containers

◀ A terrace paved in concrete is the ideal setting for concrete planters. These large reinforced boxes provide space for a mix of silver and grey-leafed plants which both fit in with the material and help to soften all the hard surfaces that surround it.

▲ Square concrete pots have a simplicity that fits in with modern design. A white-flowering datura is slipped inside the square in its own plastic pot. It will look magnificent in summer and can be brought in during winter and replaced by a winter-flowering display.

available in a greater choice of shapes, from round bowls to tall cylinders. Though heavy, they are surprisingly delicate, and can easily be chipped if knocked, and their weight makes them difficult to transport. Think carefully before purchase about whether they are appropriate for your garden, and take care that they aren't too heavy if load-bearing is an issue.

In a contemporary garden, if you want to keep concrete surfaces clear of algae and moss, scrub them with a mild detergent or protect them by applying a clear stone waterproofing agent. A dry, sunny position will reduce algae and moss growth. Also, stand pale-coloured concrete containers on hard ground well away from soil, which can stain the surface. If badly stained, concrete can be covered with a coat of masonry paint.

When drilling drainage holes in concrete, be patient. Use a masonry or ceramic drill bit, and place the rim of the container on a soft surface to allow a bit of "give". After planting I like to cover the soil with a mulch of gravel or glass to soften the hard edges of the container.

can help to establish a garden that really fits in with its urban surroundings.

Strong materials like concrete benefit from simple and bold plantings. Grasses have a particular affinity with concrete containers, particularly the blue-grey foliage of *Festuca glauca*, the powerful thrust of phormium, and I also love the silver of *Euphorbia myrsinites*. The silvery grey foliage of teucrium with its sky blue flowers will help to break up the hard line of a concrete container edge, as will the silvery feathered leaves of cineraria or a gold grass like hakonechloa.

More recently, concrete containers have become

◀ A little imagination and these concrete circles are transformed. A couple of bands of copper wire around these containers give them an individual look. They also help to visually link the container with the flooring, which is made of rusting steel panels.

◀◀ A concrete courtyard with huge concrete containers gives the impression of permanence. This is a valuable, stable material for busy areas, and when planting long-term large specimen trees and hedges.

▶ A bespoke concrete pot individually made shows purple and pink clouds and is a really special feature in the garden. The red-leafed phormium appears like a fountain of foliage.

METHOD

• This large concrete container is heavy so make sure that there are two of you to carry it.

• Drill drainage holes in the base of the container with a masonry bit and place crocks in the bottom.

• Fill up half of this deep container with pieces of polystyrene and infill with soil-based compost. Try to shake the soil down between the gaps in the polystyrene pieces.

• Plant up the container at any time of year. Place the choisya and lamium so that they sit about 1cm (½in) below the rim of the pot.

• Feed with seaweed fertilizer.

• Cut back lamium when it gets leggy. Trim the choisya once it has flowered to maintain the plant's compact bush shape. Eventually the choisya may take over the whole pot.

shade-loving companions

This arrangement looks good in a modern setting and its fresh appearance helps to lift a shady area of the garden. I think the smooth surface of the concrete creates a good foil for the foilage, and the golden hue of the choisya leaves is exaggerated when set against this pale concrete surface. *Choisya ternata* 'Sundance', a slow-growing compact evergreen shrub, occupies centre-stage. It produces attractive white flowers in early summer, and glossy golden foliage all year round. Take care as very hot sun may scorch the foliage. The choisya is underplanted with *Lamium maculatum* 'Beacon Silver'.

PLANTING MATERIALS

Tall concrete container

Crocks

Broken polystyrene or similar lightweight filler

Soil-based compost

PLANTS

Choisya ternata 'Sundance'

Lamium maculatum 'Beacon Silver'

PLANT ALTERNATIVES

Choisya ternata 'Goldfinger'

Escallonia 'Gold Brian'

Jasminum 'Fiona Sunrise'

Vinca major

Vinca minor 'Variegata'

metal

The new generation of large planters is dominated by those made of metal, and new designs and finishes help the gardener to achieve contemporary effects and create lovely gardens where there is little natural soil.

The variety of metal containers available to the gardener has expanded dramatically in recent years. They used to be quite expensive and rare, and the choice limited. However, the new designs are simple and understated, creating a range of planters that are helping to define the small, modern garden.

The boom in high-rise living and apartments with balconies and roof gardens seems to have fuelled homeowner's interest in stylish metal containers. The value put on any private space means that people are more keen to use any outdoor space they have for eating and entertaining. Metal containers are one of the lightest planters available, so are ideal for situations where load-bearing may be an issue.

I think fashionable home furnishing shops have also encouraged the use of metal fixtures and fittings for both inside and out, and metal containers match the current enthusiasm for a minimalist approach. Galvanised containers fit in well with the architectural detailing of many of the newer buildings which often use metal in their construction.

The natural sheen on metal containers actually helps to boost and reflect light opening up these limited spaces. Reflected light on a balcony is subtle but important. Garden lighting has also created new opportunities, and the reflections off metal surfaces creates some interesting effects at night, adding a new dimension to the idea of a garden being an outdoor room.

▶ Very modern floating stainless-steel containers filled with grasses like this lovely bronze *Carex comans* look like lily pads. The reflections of the metal in the water makes this material particularly appropriate in a modern garden setting.

▶▶ These huge containers are relatively light when empty and are easy to carry. Metal looks natural in a space that is surrounded by buildings and sky and against the glass doors of a modern apartment.

◀ Smart galvanised metal boxes make excellent planters for some of the more vigorous bamboos, like *Phyllostachys nigra*, the black-stemmed bamboo. The dark sheen of the stem looks stunning emerging from a pebble mulch and the shiny galvanised metal.

Some metal planters mimic traditional pot shapes, but I think that these are less attractive than the simple squares, rectangles and circles.

Different metal finishes are available and the most common and appropriate for garden containers is galvanised metal, which offers protection against metal decay and rust, and is both lightweight and strong. Darker burnished metal finishes are now available, and these give the container a slightly older, more antiqued appearance. Stainless-steel is a heavier and more expensive alternative.

Large metal containers also provide one of the most cost-effective ways of introducing plenty of soil and plants into an area that has no soil without major upheaval. Large-scale metal planters give the gardener wonderful planting opportunities – a metal rectangle 90 x 40cm (36 x 16in) is ideal for growing climbers like jasmine, solanum and even wisteria in a large volume of soil.

As a base that offsets the plants, metal pots can look unique. Choosing a plant that complements the colour of the metal is the key. Silvery foliage in galvanised metal can create a real focal point, while variegated thyme, pittosporum and myrtle leaves also look attractive grown in metal pots. White flowers appear clean and strong, and a shrub like *Cistus corbariensis* will mound to form a really substantial plant, with delicate white flowers and delightful aromatic foliage. Bamboos look thoroughly at home in metal, particularly the dark-stemmed *Phyllostachys nigra* when some of the bottom green leaves are stripped back to reveal the extraordinary lacquered black stems. Stick with the principle of bold and simple, but do not be afraid to experiment with new combinations. A large phormium looks stunning planted with some dark red nasturtiums like 'Empress of India' and the feathery silvers of santolina or some of the new lavenders. Olives are a natural partner for the galvanised containers as their

leaves have a metallic sheen. Matching the colour tones of metal is challenging and fun, think of the metallic steel of an astelia, the silvery *Senecio* 'Sunshine'. I also love the yellow and green evergreen leaves of the grass *Carex* 'Evergold', helichrysum and the weird tight foliage of the whipcord hebe (*Hebe lycipodioides*). But avoid using metal containers with plants in a wide range of colours – a reflective metal base planted up with a kaleidoscope of colours looks too dazzling.

Modern metal containers can fit anywhere but look particularly good in gardens which have plenty of hard surfaces on view. The burnished planter often looks more appropriate in a natural setting, for instance a cottage garden where there are more blurred edges – plants mingling with plants, informal shapes breaching the sky – where the darker finish feels far more at home than the shiny precision of galvanised metal. My own garden is a more eclectic mix and I have found

▲ A cluster of white agapanthus in an old metal tub are a magnificent display in the summer and help to create interest in this small garden. One really good-sized container, filled with a single species often makes the most effective and dramatic planting.

galvanised containers a great addition to my landscape, fitting in perfectly well with terracotta, concrete and stone pots.

Copper planters are beautiful when they age, developing a verdigris patina, but these are difficult to find and expensive. More traditional planters made of lead are wonderful but rarely available. If you are lucky enough to find one they are worth cherishing but remember they are phenomenally heavy. Here the actual metal container should take the starring role while the planting is used solely to show off the container. Wirework containers that need a moss lining before they can be planted up can still be bought, though more often than not from old gardening shops.

Double-skinned metal containers are available and these are quite useful in extreme weather conditions as they provide some insulation against either heat or cold. However, I would suggest that in areas with really hot sun or freezing winters it is worth lining metal pots with polystyrene or bubble-wrap to insulate the soil and protect the roots. Any permanent planter would benefit from this insulation, particularly as unseasonal weather conditions are now more commonplace. Drainage as always is essential and most metal planters do not come with drainage holes, so drill out the base with a metal bit, and if lining the container with bubble-wrap make sure that there are holes in this plastic liner.

▶ A majestic mature *Agave americana* complements the verdigris of a copper pot creating a partnership that shows off both the planter and the plant to their best effect. Matching the textures and shades of colour can create a display like a living garden sculpture.

▶▶ A small galvanised container planted with the autumn-flowering *Gentiana sino-ornata* makes a stunning display just as most of the garden is preparing to go to sleep. A planting like this is effective because of its sheer simplicity.

METHOD

• Ensure that there is good drainage and fill up the whole of this container with an equal mix of peat-free multi-purpose and soil-based compost.

• Plant out in mid- to late spring in a sheltered position.

• Sweet peas are quite hungry plants, and also dislike drying out. Keep well watered and feed regularly from midsummer (when they start producing an abundance of flowers) with a liquid seaweed feed.

• Plant the nasturtiums around the edge of the metal container. Deadhead the plants to encourage masses of flowers.

• Keep in a sunny position to produce the optimum number of flowers.

tower of flowers

I like the informality of this display, masses of flowers and a lot of height and volume for a container-based planting. The proportions of this arrangement work well with the depth of the metal cylinder balancing the height of the wigwam. Sweet peas (*Lathyrus odoratus*) are amongst the most productive of flowering plants – the more flowers you pick the more are produced. Nasturtium flowers (*Tropaeolum majus*), in clashing oranges and yellows, spill out over the edge of the planter and flower with an intensity equal to the sweet peas. Black-eyed Susan (*Thunbergia alata*) would be a good alternative twining climber with yellow flowers and dark centres, while *Tropaeolum* Alaska Series would make a striking substitute for *T. majus*.

PLANTING MATERIALS

Tall metal container

Crocks

Mix of soil-based compost and peat-free multi-purpose compost

PLANTS

Lathyrus odoratus

Tropaeolum majus

PLANT ALTERNATIVES

Ipomoea coccinea

Thunbergia alata

Tropaeolum Alaska Series

A quirky container made out of a very wide piece of bamboo, makes an interesting and surprising temporary display for a plant like golden everlasting (*Bracteantha bracteata*).

wood

One of the most traditional materials for containers, wood tends to be overlooked by the modern gardener as being too old-fashioned. However, natural or painted wood planters in simple shapes can hold their own in a contemporary setting.

The most traditional style of wooden containers are Versailles tubs, named after the palace south of Paris where in the seventeenth century they were used to grow exotics which were brought into the greenhouse in winter for protection. I associate this style with formal traditional plantings of bay and box topiary but these tubs can make surprisingly good planters in modern gardens. The main reason is that they are very adaptable, easy to stain or paint, and work well as an outer decorative pot for less attractive plastic containers.

Containers like these made of softwoods such as pine are good value. However, softwood, unless it has been pressure treated to preserve it, is prone to rot particularly in damper garden climates, so protect containers with a coat of wood preservative or paint. I often use wood stains and paints to help redecorate an area of my garden, particularly as my raised beds have been constructed using wooden gravel boards. To create a harmonious effect throughout the garden, the same paint colour can be used on a range of wooden containers. The grain

of wood itself is an attribute and many stains allow the grain to show through.

Another advantage of wooden containers is that they provide reasonably good insulation for roots in very cold climates. Wood is also worth considering if you want to make your own containers. Making large containers is easy, though once built, I tend to treat them as immovable objects as soon as they have been filled with soil and planted up. Ordinary preserved softwood is perfectly adequate though using old, sun-bleached wood (similar to beach driftwood) with its silvered tones and splits can give

▲ Versailles tubs are traditional formal planters ideal for plants like these tightly clipped lavender. Staining wood, in this case grey-green, is one of the easiest ways to match the container to other garden features.

▶ A large wooden planter is big enough to house a specimen mature birch tree. Because of its weight, it is best to install the square planter in its permanent position when empty.

◀ A hardwood planter with beautiful grain makes a contemporary statement in this small courtyard garden. The compact pine works well as it does not cover up the wood surface. The use of old railway sleepers against the wall helps to link the planter with the rest of the garden design.

real character to a space, particularly if it has a seaside theme. It can also add character to a modern space. Large hollowed-out bamboo makes for a quirky, and surprisingly long-lasting, watertight container.

Beer barrels are now specially made for container planting, and are useful particularly in busy areas where the container may need to be hard-wearing, for instance in driveways or at entrance and exit points to the house. They are also heavy and will hold steady in exposed or windy sites. When buying a wooden barrel check that the metal hoops are well fastened around the girth of the barrel, as when wood dries out it tends to contract. I have seen the hoops slip off and a barrel fall apart. Also make sure that there are adequately large drainage holes, at least 1cm (2.5in) in diameter, and that the inside of the barrel is burnt or treated with wood preservative to stop it rotting from the inside out.

To prevent beer barrels looking like those seen in British pub gardens, it is worth taking real care when planting them. I prefer to use the really large barrels, and plant them with something that can compete with their bulky proportions. Trees look good in barrels, partly because a strong trunk coming out of a wood base is like a horticultural sculpture. The beautiful *Prunus subhirtella* 'Autumnalis' has just the right balance to keep the display looking in proportion, or the beautiful bark of the paper-bark maple, *Acer griseum*.

There are some sophisticated hardwood containers, like dark iroko, that are quite beautiful though they are expensive and quite tricky to find. Wooden sleeves to cover up plastic window boxes are also a good idea to improve the appearance of the house entrance. There are also forms of woodland split log containers which are good value but short-lived.

▼ With the increased use of timber decking on terraces it seems natural to use timber planters. These are like miniature raised beds planted full of herbs and are a simple and effective extension of the decked patio area.

METHOD

• Store the wood barrel outside before use to keep the wood slightly damp which will help to prevent the planted-up display from drying out.

• Drill drainage holes at least 2.5cm (1in) in diameter.

• Put in a layer of crocks and fill the container with soil-based compost.

• A mature tree sold in a container will almost certainly be root-bound. Remove the birch from its pot, and pull apart the roots with your fingers to separate them out before planting the tree in the barrel. Water it in and mulch to suppress weeds and preserve moisture.

• In late winter or early spring, plant primulas and snowdrops at the base of the tree for extra interest.

• The snowdrops will reappear each winter, and the clumps of primulas can be propagated by division in autumn and replanted if there is space in the barrel.

woodland copse

I like the way the white bark of the birch matches the painted wooden barrel. Not only is this large tree firmly planted in soil-based compost but visually anchored as well. This display highlights the value of growing a larger specimen in a container, helping to create instant height and vertical interest in an outdoor setting. The bark of the birch takes at least five years to show its beauty, so I think it's worth buying a mature tree for immediate impact. The snowdrops and primulas transform this planting into a miniature woodland scene that can be recreated in even a small courtyard. Plant primulas and snowdrops in autumn to flower in late winter and early spring.

PLANTING MATERIALS

Large wooden barrel (unvarnished)

Exterior white paint for wood

Crocks

Soil-based compost

Gravel mulch

PLANTS

Betula jacquemontii (Himalayan birch)

Galanthus nivalis (snowdrop)

Primula 'Gold lace'

PLANT ALTERNATIVES

Betula ermanii (white-barked birch)

Betula pendula 'Youngii' (small-growing weeping birch)

Leucojum vernum

Primula vulgaris

recycled

Finding recycled containers is fun, rewarding and good for the environment. A good recycled container can look marvellous in the garden and creates a really lovely display that adds an imaginative and unique edge to outdoor areas.

Part of the pleasure of container gardening is the hunt for attractive pots but nothing measures up to the excitement of finding good recycled containers. With a little imagination, an old piece of junk can be transformed into a beautiful home for a plant and you can feel satisfied that you have combined caring for the environment and your bank balance with creating your own unique display.

Many of the best recycled containers started out life as containers for either storing or transporting food and drink such as the large attractive tins used to import marinated olives and olive oil and the wooden crates used to carry some of the more expensive wines. It is a good idea to plant up these recycled containers with something that reminds you of the origins of the product. Lavender works really well in old tins and wooden wine boxes as do trailing geraniums as both these plants are seen growing in almost every village throughout the Mediterranean region.

In my opinion, the more delicious the product the more attractive the container is to reuse in the garden. I like to use wine boxes printed with the words Chianti, Chateau or Burgundy – all make delightful guests in the garden on a summer's evening and what could be more appropriate than containers originally used for transporting food being used to grow edible plants? In my own garden, an aubergine lives happily

in a large olive container, while old tins of tomatoes are planted up with miniature tomato plants. Because recycled containers introduce mood, texture and colour to the garden, planting them up is fun and can be quite challenging. A really attractive rusty pot can be combined with rusty coloured foliage, like *Heuchera* 'Chocolate Ruffles' or *H.* 'Plum Pudding'. These simple associations between a pot and plant also ensure that the display doesn't become confusing.

With most recycled containers, particularly wooden ones, it is worth remembering that their life is limited to a few years. Wood usually needs treating, and the application of a colourless preservative will help a wine box last longer in the garden. But the boxes were not built to hold the weight of wet soil, or to be exposed to the elements for months on end. Also, metal naturally rusts, though oiling it with a natural oil can help to preserve its good

looks. Otherwise, lining metal containers with bubble-wrap (*see Materials: Metal page 68*) will prolong their life.

Illusion and fantasy can be explored to the limits when using recycled containers and by mixing in a few other quirky recycled ornaments. Towards the back of my garden, an old tea chest that I found in a skip makes a good home with ample room for a large evergreen shrub while a length of old chain, cockle shells, and seaside plants

▲ A real gem like this unusual pig feeder is worth showing off, not only for its beauty as a planter but because of its history. People like to guess its original use (they are always wrong) and planted with a mix of culinary herbs it is a beautiful and useful addition to the garden.

in old weathered terracotta pots gives my garden a maritime feel even though it is situated in the heart of north London. Reclaimed wooden planks and sleepers extend into the area and I have treated the wood with a blow torch to give it a scorched, sun-bleached appearance. I think this helps to fuse the seaside elements with the rest of the garden.

Used carefully, illusion can really work well. I prefer to hint at feelings, and not try to show them in full. Somehow attempting a complete seaside scene in my

small urban paradise would seem too improbable. I've seen upturned boats in an urban setting and they just look out of place.

Unfortunately collecting used containers can become addictive. The more you look the more you find, and I have discovered to my cost that delicatessens and restaurants are always delighted to off-load their used catering-sized tins! Though it's lovely having such an eclectic mix of planters, take care not to overdo it or the garden will end up looking like a scrap yard. Also in winter, when the plants have died back, the empty containers can appear a little forlorn and there is no question that a poorly maintained garden with recycled containers looks more shabby than other garden styles.

Though found objects can fit in with most designs, the smaller the space and the more strictly themed that space is, the more care you need to take. An old object in a small garden can really stand out and become a focal point that can detract from the design as a whole. Make these containers more low-key and less prominent, and make sure that they merge well into the surrounding landscape.

unusual recycled containers

There are more sophisticated recycled containers but often these are quite expensive items to buy. Some are really beautiful and become a real feature, like an old metal washbasin, even a cattle trough makes for a beautiful container. Plant these up to highlight the container and do not obscure it by choosing to grow trailing plants. Chimney pots made of clay make a beautiful ornament in most styles of garden whether formal or informal. I like the simple terracotta chimney pots that are free of ornamentation. They are quite challenging to plant up because they are tall and narrow. My own favourites for these unusual containers are plants like *Convolvulus cneorum* or *Thymus* 'Silver Queen' which produce a shimmering silver effect. They grow best in a sunny site in well-drained soil.

preparing recycled containers

All recycled containers will need to be thoroughly cleaned on the inside before use so that the soil does not become contaminated. Wearing rubber gloves, scrub the insides with a mild disinfectant solution. When dry, drill several drainage holes in the base so that the soil can drain freely and the roots of the plants do not become waterlogged. (*see Care page 132*).

◀ Food containers, like this enamel storage tin, make great recycled planters, in this case for a planting of a mizuma salad. Food containers always look far more at home in the garden than recycled containers which were used for manufactured goods.

▼ An olive tin from the local delicatessen makes an attractive planter for a fern, bringing a bit of French culture into an urban garden. I like to highlight the beauty of the pot by matching up the metal grooves on the tin with the patterns of the foliage.

METHOD

• Drill the container with a metal bit and make sure that you create at least six large holes because courgettes are quite thirsty and greedy plants.

• Use an equal mix of soil-based compost and a little well-rotted manure, and add some well-rotted manure to the ground under the container.

• Plant out the courgettes in spring after the danger of frost has passed, in a sunny or semi-shady position, and mulch the surface to help conserve moisture.

• Water well and feed once the plant is established. The courgette will not grow as big as one grown in a larger container or in the ground, but it will still fruit well.

• The container should help to protect the courgette plant from slug attack. Vigilance and copper tape under the rim of the pot can also help.

pot-grown produce

This is a real eye-catching display that makes people smile and serves up some lovely fresh vegetables. This recipe shows the value of the flexibility of containers, using them in an existing bed to add another layer of interest. The coloured mulch not only keeps moisture in but also looks great against the blue of the recycled metal bucket. In spring, plant out the nasturtiums in the raised bed close to the metal pot. These are wonderfully hardy and will trail across the border as well as mingling with the bright yellow courgette flowers and fruit.

PLANTING
MATERIALS

Recycled metal
bucket

1 part soil-based
compost to 1 part
well-rotted manure

Mulch of dyed
broken shells

PLANTS

Golden-skinned
courgette (Goldrush
or Jemmer F1)

PLANT ALTERNATIVES

Chilli pepper

Sweet pepper

Strawberries

woven

Traditionally, woven wicker has been associated with rustic country-style gardens but new designs and shapes have helped to update its image and make woven containers an attractive choice for the modern garden.

Hazel and willow poles woven into fence panels and flower bed edgings make attractive borders for gardens, while containers made from these natural materials can introduce a relaxed feel to a city space. In my own garden I have some old woven containers under the stag's horn sumach tree (*Rhus typhina*), where I can go and switch off from the telephone and fax machine and just listen to the birds singing.

Like woven fence panels and edgings, wicker containers are made from the flexible branches of willow or hazel but more often than not they are woven into traditional basket shapes. But the flexibility and strength of the raw material has encouraged people to experiment with more imaginative designs that look more like modern sculpture than plant holders.

preparing woven containers

I like to use woven planters as a more attractive outer covering for arrangements planted up in plastic pots. Like other wood containers, woven hazel or willow are prone to rot if they come into contact with damp soil or compost. To protect the weave, paint the inside of the basket with a clear wood preservative and then line the container with polythene sheeting, cut down to size and stapled to hold it in place. (Some now come ready fitted with an in-built plastic lining.) Pierce the plastic sheet a few times along the bottom to make sure that there is adequate drainage. During the winter months

or when they are not in use, try and keep woven containers dry by bringing them indoors or storing them in a garden shed. Keep the container off the ground so that it stays as damp-free as possible.

I really enjoy the relaxing feeling of having a purely organic-looking container. It is the nearest thing to having nature create a pot for you. Rather like a bird's nest made of twigs and leaves, a woven container can look really wholesome. They are ideal for a bit of seasonal colour, partly because they don't look like a permanent fixture. A collection of busy lizzies or cyclamen in the shade, a larger *Impatiens* New Guinea Group hybrid in a basket, or even a *Fuchsia* 'Thalia' dripping with orange flowers looks completely at home in a woven container. I also like to use plants that combine with the strong horizontal lines of the weave, like tall grasses, ferns and astilbe, which seem to celebrate life by exploding into the air.

Larger homemade woven containers can be created by fixing together a small framework of softwood, onto which you can attach small panels of hazel or willow hurdles. This can act as a simple and attractive outer sleeve for plants already growing in plastic pots. It is still worth lining the inside of the woven planter with polythene to help prevent rotting and a mulch of moss gives it a real country feel.

◀ This woven container has a rustic air, nestling between established plants and planted so that the shades of brown pansies match the painted wood.

▲ Hazel hurdles within a wooden frame bring nature to a corner of the garden. The hazel fencing panel behind shows the value of integrating the container with its surroundings.

METHOD

• Preserve the weave with a clear horticultural wood preservative (there are specific ones for garden use) and plant up when the container is completely dry.

• Line the container with polythene sheeting to prevent the soil from coming into direct contact with the weave. Pierce the polythene and line it with vermiculite or gravel to ensure good drainage.

• Plant in a peat-free multi-purpose compost or, if there is room, plunge the plants in their existing plastic pots into the container.

• Mulch the soil surface with chipped stones to prevent damp soil sticking to the container during watering.

• Do not overwater the plant material as all of these species can survive quite happily in dry conditions.

• Cut off the old leaves from the phormium with scissors, and clip back the ajuga after it has flowered. If grown in its plastic pot, the ajuga will benefit from being divided in the autumn of the second year.

modern weave

This container with its sleek and modern shape helps to break away from the usual stereotype of a woven container. The mix of coloured grasses and phormium create a lovely balanced display that would fit into most patio areas and it will continue to look good all year round. Grasses are extremely versatile and easy to manage and they grow well in the confines of a container. They provide the amateur or professional gardener with a wonderful choice of texture and colour.

PLANTING MATERIALS

Woven container

Polythene sheeting

Peat-free multi-purpose compost

Mulch of chipped stones

PLANTS

Phormium 'Bronze Baby'

Ajuga purpurea

Carex 'Evergold'

Acorus gramineus 'Ogon'

PLANT ALTERNATIVES

Cordyline australis

Festuca glauca

Phormium tenax 'Maori Maiden'

synthetics

Unfortunately, some of the gaudy plastic and poorly designed fibreglass containers have given all synthetics a bad name. However, many still offer real value and can make a modern contribution to the container garden.

◀ A group of fibreglass pots can create a fun atmosphere in the garden, and planted with easy colourful plants like chrysanthemum and kalanchoe are a real kids' favourite.

▶ A double sunflower (*Helianthus annuus* 'Teddy Bear') provides a jolly splash of colour and always makes me smile. In many ways sunflowers are ideal for a large plastic container that doesn't take itself too seriously.

Synthetic containers are those made of plastic or fibreglass. Plastic pots are incredibly light, can be very good value and are easy to find. Though most people wouldn't be boasting about their new plastic pot, they certainly have a place in the garden.

My favourite are the industrial black pots used by most nurseries to grow plants. What you see is what you get and I like this utilitarian simplicity. They are not pretending to be faux terracotta or any other material, they are just good value, effective containers. My own garden is full of recently bought unplanted specimens, and the black plastic containers fit quite happily into the design. The larger plastic containers also have handles so they can be moved about easily. Sun, however, tends to degrade plastic so these containers have a limited life of about five years. Coloured plastic containers are more difficult to fit into a garden scheme, but look quite jolly when placed in a group in a courtyard or on a table top.

Imitation terracotta plastic pots are heavy duty, and are a good alternative to the real thing as they will not break or chip. Their light weight makes them suitable for roof gardens and balconies but take care in windy sites or when planting them up with tall specimens. On the downside, plastic does not age well like terracotta.

Fibreglass planters are a good investment, in particular some of the lead- and metal-effect imitations that take a historic trough design and make it available at an affordable price. I have been fooled into believing that lead-effect fibreglass planters are the real thing, though poorly made ones can look dreadful. Large, bespoke containers can be commissioned from some boat builders who work in fibreglass, and can be a stylish, if expensive, way of bringing extra plants into a garden where flower bed space is limited.

In a modern garden, these specially commissioned fibreglass containers have added to the choices available to the designer. Containers like this have become a key element in the design – as important as the walls and the paths – and are no longer treated only as an afterthought to be bought on impulse.

METHOD

• Drill a hole slowly in the fibreglass, taking care not to put too much pressure on the material. Use crocks to create adequate drainage and plant into a soil-based compost.

• Feed with general purpose fertilizer, though neither of these species need much pampering.

• In the autumn, a couple of seasons on, take out the heuchera and divide the plants. Return only half the plants to the display with a bit of fresh compost.

• Top-dress the pot with new compost with a handful of bonemeal mixed in to feed the pine tree roots.

sculptural spikes

I think that pine trees make wonderful container plants and create an instantly modern feel. I particularly like this design set against a plain background. I deliberately chose a standard pine for this display. This species is *Pinus nigra* which has relatively large needles and a relaxed shape. There are plenty of pines that would look just as good. Choose slow-growing, compact species that will not outgrow the pot too quickly. Pines are very adaptable, and fit well in all sorts of difficult environments such as windy, exposed sites. To create an attractive carpet of foliage at the base of the pine, I have used *Heuchera* 'Silver Scrolls'. This excellent plant has a fascinating veined leaf. The new range of heucheras is amazing, they are semi-evergreen and there are plenty of colour variations to choose from.

PLANTING MATERIALS

Fibreglass container

Crocks

Soil-based compost

PLANTS

Standard *Pinus nigra*

Heuchera 'Silver Scrolls'

PLANT ALTERNATIVES

Laurus nobilis (bay) or *Olea europea* (olive)

Heuchera 'Plum Pudding' and 'Chocolate Ruffles' are darker-leafed forms or 'Amber Waves' a gold form.

PLANTING MATERIALS

Lead-effect fibreglass container

Gravel

Equal mix of soil-based compost and peat-free multi-purpose compost

PLANTS

Buxus sempervirens (trained into a ball)

Curly-leafed parsley (*Petroselinum crispum*)

PLANT ALTERNATIVES

Ligustrum

Buxus sempervirens 'Suffruticosa'

METHOD

• Drill a hole slowly in the fibreglass, taking care not to put too much pressure on the material.

• Place a layer of gravel in the pot base and plant in an equal mix of soil-based compost and peat-free multi-purpose compost.

• Autumn is a good time to buy a topiary box ball. Try buying one from a nursery with the root ball wrapped in hessian sacking rather than already planted in a pot as they are far better value.

• Remove the sacking and soak the root ball for at least 10 minutes before planting.

• Plant curly-leafed parsley (*Petroselinum crispum*) in all four corners of the square planter. Alternatively, use slow-growing *Buxus sempervirens* 'Suffruticosa' in the corners instead of parsley.

fresh green square

This display shows the power and range of greens – the most restful of horticultural colours. Parsley is a wonderfully lush foliage plant and produces a sea of green from which the box emerges. I bought the curly-leafed parsley in 1.5-litre pots and, when established in early summer, sank them into the four corners of the display. Keep the parsley well watered and fed with a foliar feed and it will crop until autumn, and in winter during mild spells. Replace the plants when the parsley runs to seed the following year. Remove yellow leaves, and move the display in summer, as parsley likes a little shade. In autumn, top-dress with compost and bonemeal.

site

sun

Planted containers can really glow in the warmth of the sun, thriving in high temperatures and increased light levels. Choose sun-loving plants, and a great pot and you will be rewarded by magnificent displays of flowers and foliage throughout the summer.

South-facing walls, sunny borders and bright blue skies are the perfect stage setting for many pot-grown plants, especially those that are native to the Mediterranean and Africa. Not only colours but fragrances become more intense in bright sunshine and the garden feels more vital and alive.

Many of the finest sun-loving plants, including figs, vines and olives grow well when their roots are confined, making them ideal candidates for containers. In their natural habitat, these plants can seem to grow out of pure rock. I have seen huge, ancient olives in giant containers and an antique vine with its stem gnarled and twisted growing happily in an old wine barrel. Figs undoubtedly fruit better when their roots are restricted, limiting leaf growth and encouraging bud formation.

Luckily we are spoilt for choice when it comes to choosing container plants that like a sunny site. For large-scale plantings, choose trees and shrubs like

▶ Huge terracotta pots of *Convolvulus cneorum* flower magnificently when grown in a well-drained, gritty soil in full sun.

▶▶ An aeonium bakes in the heat of the day. These fleshy-leafed plants can withstand both high temperatures and drought.

◀ This agapanthus almost bursts out of its container and is one of the most rewarding of sun-loving plants. They seem to flower even more profusely when their roots are confined in a pot and they help to give this small garden a classical Italian feeling.

▲ Oleander is a plant that we're accustomed to seeing growing in the South of France. Planted in a container in a sheltered garden site it can look wonderful and evocative. In cold areas move the pot inside during winter.

▶ Nasturtiums are easy to grow and keep flowering well into autumn. These sunny orange and yellow flowers create a dazzling display that literally glows in the sun.

bay or eucalyptus or the magnificent evergreen *Magnolia grandiflora* with its huge glossy leaves, and heavily scented flowers. There are also surprises – the bamboo is usually considered a moisture-loving plant, but I have found that *Phyllostachys nigra* and *P. aurea* can grow huge in a large container in the sun. There are a number of different pines that are wonderful grown in pots and give off that fresh resinous aroma. When potting up young plants that grow tall, make sure that the pot is large enough to hold the mature plant.

Many of the aromatic plants, often associated with the Mediterranean region, like lavenders, thyme, cistus, sage and phlomis, appear to produce more flowers, more intense aromas, and a better leaf colour when grown in pots in sunny sites. These herbs thrive in the sun and when their aromatic foliage is warmed, the fragrant oils in the leaves rise to the surface and increase their scent and flavour. In my own garden the bay tree that occupies the slightly shady position in fertile open ground is a huge, dark green giant with insipid-flavoured leaves, while the one restricted to a pot produces far better leaves for cooking. Many other herbs like to bake in the sun, including tarragon, basil and mint and their leaves taste stronger as a result.

Most of the grey-leafed plants, like lavender, *Convolvulus cneorum*, santolina and artemisia are adapted for growing in hot conditions. The huge range of lavenders now available at nurseries provides the container gardener with an overwhelming choice of plants. Though the exquisite *Lavandula stoechas* types (French lavenders) are less hardy than *L. angustifolia*, I think they are worth growing. Use a free-draining compost and place in the hottest, most sheltered site in the garden. Their roots hate sitting in wet, poorly drained compost, particularly in winter, so I add a bit of gravel and vermiculite to the compost mix to improve the drainage.

Vegetables that originated in warmer climates, chilli

peppers, aubergines and tomatoes positively glow when brought out into the sun but during propagation and cold spells they must be kept indoors or in a greenhouse. Containers provide the gardener with the opportunity to really maximize the amount of sun a plant can absorb, as the pot can follow the sun. My own south-facing terrace is cast in shadow by the middle of the summer because of a large overhanging tree so I often move my pot-grown vegetables into the sunniest place during the growing season so that they have a chance to ripen. My aubergines start in a protected corner site, and always end up by late summer on the edge of the pond where the sun spends much of the day.

Many bedding and patio plants thrive in containers in the sun, producing a blaze of colour. Every season there are new varieties available which promise even greater flower production. In the sun, verbenas, diascias, osteospermums, bidens, and argyranthemums flower to exhaustion. More traditional bedding plants like petunias, geraniums and marigolds also perform amazingly well and their colours seem to positively vibrate in the sunshine.

In gardens where pots may have to go without water during a hot spell, choose plants that are drought-resistant. Select those with succulent leaves like sempervivums, and sedums or some of the alpines. Palms with waxy foliage, trachycarpus, aeoniums, phormiums, cordylines, yuccas, and most of the ornamental grasses are the most drought-tolerant. A mulch (*see Care, page 134*) will reduce evaporation from the soil surface, and if you are going away consider installing an irrigation system.

Strangely plants in pots often suffer in dry, warm spells in winter because we assume that they have enough water and have stopped growing. Peat-based soils dry out quickly, and when dry are difficult to rehydrate. Water simply drains through the pot so it needs to be soaked by standing the pot in water. Soil-based compost is better in that it dries out more slowly.

▶ *Festuca glauca*, phormium, stipa and many other grasses enjoy being baked in the sun and are relatively drought-tolerant. I like to create a beach effect with some driftwood and cobble stones mixed in with the containers and gravel.

▶▶ *Senecio cineraria* is one of my favourite sun-lovers. It is easy to grow and very much associated with the seaside. Grow this silvery shrub in a large container so that it can develop into an attractive mound.

▶▶▶ Here, purple sage is planted in an old French olive jar. I like the contrast between the warm ochre colour of the pot with the soft purple tones of the sage leaves.

METHOD

• Drill drainage holes and line the inside of the metal container with bubble-wrap for insulation to prevent the plant roots from frying in hot sun.

• Pierce holes in the bubble-wrap along the base of the container and add a fine layer of gravel for drainage.

• To keep the soil free-draining (lavender roots hate sitting in water) add a scoop of horticultural grit to the soil-based potting compost.

• When planting lavender, gently tease the roots free of the main root ball to give them access to fresh soil.

• Water the container regularly throughout the spring and summer to prevent the plants from drying out. If you are going on holiday and watering is a problem move the container to a shady site.

• Cut the lavender hard back after flowering, which will help stop the plants from becoming leggy and woody in subsequent years. Feed with flowering food in the growing season. Deadhead the violas, and trim back cineraria when necessary.

mediterranean metal

I like the silver-grey colour and the soft texture of this display, which looks in keeping with the surface sheen of the galvanised metal planter. The centre of the display is planted with *Lavandula stoechas*, which I like for its butterfly-winged flowers, aromatic foliage and feathery look. Delicate violas provide colour along the edge, and when glimpsed through the silver foliage of the cineraria bind the window box display together with a colourful thread.

PLANTING MATERIALS

Galvanised metal
window box

Bubble-wrap

Gravel

Horticultural grit

Soil-based compost

PLANTS

Lavandula stoechas

Cineraria maritima

Viola

PLANT ALTERNATIVES

Lavandula angustifolia
'Hidcote' or 'Imperial Gem'

Helichrysum petiolare

Lobelia

PLANTING MATERIALS

Glazed stoneware pot about 22cm (9in) in diameter at the rim

Crocks

Peat-free multi-purpose compost

PLANTS

Capsicum annuum
Culinary cultivars bear hot-tasting, conical fruit 5cm (2in) long.

Viola 'Panola'

PLANT ALTERNATIVES

Capsicum annuum 'Apache' (performs well as compact bush and good fruiter)

Any *Viola* species

METHOD

• Drill holes in the bottom of the stoneware container and add terracotta crocks to help the drainage.

• Buy the capsicum plants mid-season when the weather has warmed up as they are frost tender.

• Plant this display in a peat-free multi-purpose compost and feed throughout the season. (Capsicum grow best in fertile, well-drained soil in full sun.)

• Put the container planting in as sunny a place as possible to encourage the green capsicum fruit to ripen, and water twice a day.

• Deadhead the viola flowers and pinch them out when they get straggly to encourage more flowers.

• Pick the red fruit of an edible capsicum when fully coloured and use to add a hot spicy flavour to cooking.

sunshine spice

This display indulges the uninhibited pleasure of mixing plants that you would not normally associate with one another. Here, I have kept to basic colour principles, making sure that the scarlet and purple tones of the ripening fruit, and soft grey hue of the container all work well together, with some powerful red highlights to spark it up. Somehow I find a small display like this liberating. It enables you to get away from the more "usual" container-grown plants, and growing an edible capsicum in a pot, on a windowsill or patio, gives you a spicy culinary ingredient. Children also really love this kind of bold and colourful arrangement.

A group of mature hostas in containers is one of the most glorious displays in the garden, challenging the myth that it is difficult to grow exciting plants in shade. Hostas grow well in pots which can also help protect them from slug and snail attack.

shade

There are plenty of plants that thrive in the shade, and planted containers provide some wonderful opportunities that can help to lift and brighten an area, creating lovely effects beneath tree branches, along the edge of high walls and in dark, forgotten corners.

Shade is often considered to be the poor relation of the sun and problematic for the gardener but, in reality, there are many plants that thrive in shade and can be used to great effect. In my opinion, there are few more beautiful sights than lush green hosta leaves brimming out from terracotta pots situated in the shade, or the glossy leaves and bright flowers of a camellia emerging from a dark recess.

Many of the best results in shade can be achieved by clever use of foliage plants. The great advantage of these mainly shade-loving species is that their period of interest is longer than many of the flowering plants. An evergreen like *Pieris japonica* 'Variegata' is perfectly at home in a container and looks beautiful throughout the year. Some variegated and golden-leafed species prefer shade because their foliage gets burnt in the heat of the midday sun – the golden-leafed *Choisya* 'Sundance' prefers shady sites for this reason. Also many magnificent foliage plants, like evergreen fatsias, are far healthier when grown in diffuse light out of direct sun.

It is not only foliage but flowering plants that can excel in these shady conditions – the exquisitely scented winter flowers of *Viburnum bodnantense* and *V. fragrans* do, while *Viburnum tinus* 'Eve Price' has one of the longest flowering periods of all. One of my own favourites, *Hydrangea serrata* 'Preziosa' can grow in sun or shade, and has pink lacecaps and red-tinged foliage.

It is often plants that thrive in woodland positions that do best in the shade. Ferns, one of our most familiar woodland natives are an extraordinary group, ranging from the young emerging growth of *Matteuccia struthiopteris* (the shuttlecock fern) to the filigree foliage of soft shield fern, *Polystichum setiferum*.

The various different Japanese maples resemble a delicate lacework in the shade, and have the perfect habit for a planter, staying relatively small while retaining a tree-like shape. I made the mistake of putting a purple-leafed variety in too much sun, and the leaves got frazzled during a hot spell. Small trees like *Betula pendula* 'Youngii' can also help to brighten up a dark area.

Of the seasonal bedding plants the best container growers for shade are begonias and busy lizzies. A group of busy lizzies can brighten up the darkest corner and flower the whole summer. *Convallaria*, the lily-of-the-valley are beautiful plants for shade. Plant them out in open ground and then lift established clumps to make a display in a shallow planter.

There are degrees of shade, the dense shade cast by a sycamore or lime tree in full leaf is a problem in high summer because nothing enjoys growing under these trees, and in these hostile conditions I would recommend a really tough shade-lover like aucuba, ivy, holly or *Prunus laurocerasus*. Most shade is in fact semi-shade, and often gets 2-4 hours of sun in the summer – ideal conditions for many plants. The area under deciduous trees often has plenty of sun from the late autumn to the spring when the trees are bare, and then the leaf canopy protects the area from the summer sun. These shady environments are ideal for pots full of spring-flowering plants like snowdrops, cyclamen, primulas and bluebells, ensuring cool roots in the summer.

In shade, flowers often last longer than in full sun, so take advantage of this. One of my container-grown agapanthus which spends most of the year in the sunniest place is moved into the shade when in open bud and lasts three or four weeks longer when in flower because of the relative cool.

◀ A trio of ferns in recycled containers grow well under the dense canopy of a bamboo. Pots are useful in small beds such as this where most plants cannot compete for nutrients with bamboo.

▶ A shady woodland area in my garden is a lovely restful place that I really appreciate after a hard day. A hydrangea in a blue glazed pot flowers for weeks on end and busy lizzies are amongst the finest and most hard-working of shade-loving plants.

METHOD

• Place crocks in the pot base and fill with ericaceous compost – pieris prefers well-drained acid soil.

• Tease out the fibrous roots of the pieris to help separate out the solid rootball.

• Once planted up, use a mulch of bark to cover up the bare compost while the young plants are growing.

• Feed with sequestrine – a special food for ericaceous plants containing sequestered iron – once a season.

• Late spring frosts can damage the tender new growth of pieris. Protect the plants by covering them in horticultural fleece if a frost is forecast.

• After a couple of seasons, pot-on this display into a larger container. Remove some of the ivy, which tends to grow vigorously and take over the container.

shade-loving foliage

Shade is the perfect place for foliage arrangements, and this bright sparkling display can thrive in the gloomiest of sites. In my garden, I have placed this display close to an area where the ground is covered in ivy. It feels as though the display is in its natural home and has a permanent place, rather than just being a temporary visitor. It is often worth planting a container with something similar to what's already in the garden to help integrate it into the existing space.

PLANTING MATERIALS

Heavy duty terracotta pot

Crocks

Ericaceous compost

PLANTS

Hedera species (Trailing ivy)

Pieris japonica 'Variegata'

PLANT ALTERNATIVES

Ajuga reptans 'Rainbow'

Euonymus fortunei 'Emerald Gaiety'

Pieris japonica 'Flaming Silver'

PLANTING MATERIALS

Large glazed stoneware container

Crocks

Polystyrene filler

Equal mix of soil-based compost and peat-free multi-purpose compost

PLANTS

Fuchsia molinae (also known as *Fuchsia magellanica* 'Alba')

Impatiens hybrids

PLANT ALTERNATIVES

Fuchsia magellanica

F. magellanica 'Gracilis'

Impatiens New Guinea hybrids

METHOD

• Drill drainage holes if not already present. Half-fill this tall container with broken up pieces of polystyrene to keep it light before adding an equal mix of soil-based compost and peat-free multi-purpose compost.

• Plant the fuchsia standard and busy lizzies around the base. To keep the standard shape, keep on taking off the side shoots with your fingers as they grow up the bare stem.

• Leave the fuchsia standard to grow in the container all year round and cut it back in spring to create a tight head of flowers. Replace the busy lizzies in winter with winter-flowering pansies or cyclamen. Feed with liquid tomato feed in summer, every few weeks.

cool green planter

This fuchsia is one of my favourite plants, and has continued to thrive in my garden in a shady site. It is fully hardy and stays outside all winter. The peeling winter bark and bare stem have dramatic impact. From early summer through to autumn, it produces delicate white flowers. Planting a fuchsia in a tall glazed stone container creates height for the graceful flowers to cascade down, so that you can see them at their best. This display also shows how containers can be used in conjunction with existing plants in the garden, and I particularly like making use of the powerful verticals in the garden like the trunk of the robinia tree to the left of the main picture.

windy or exposed

Extremes of weather, particularly wind, can easily damage and dehydrate plants that are not naturally tolerant of these harsh conditions. But if you know which plants to choose and grow them in large pots that will not blow over, you can create a garden on even the windiest site.

There are plenty of plants that can tolerate gusting wind, just observe the bent-over figure of an old tree on a cliff edge or gorse flowering on a windswept beach. Plants can be incredibly tough, however, it pays to know which varieties to choose for successful results.

Wind can damage plants in a number of different ways. First there is the physical damage to buds, leaves, stems, branches or trunks and these can just break off in severe weather. In cold weather, wind can reduce the air temperature and increase the chance of wind burn and cold damage. While warm winds accelerate the rate that water is lost from plants and can cause leaves and young shoots to dry out.

Plants in containers are particularly vulnerable to physical damage because of the instability of the pot which can rock about in high winds, and as the roots

◀ A huge planter on a roof terrace provides ample room for wind-tolerant plants, with a few less hardy plants mixed in towards the middle of the display so that they are protected. Here, grasses, bamboos and phormiums help to shelter the tall stems of purple-flowering *Verbena bonariensis*.

▶ Agaves and cordylines with their strap-shaped leaves tend to be wind-resistant but need good drainage to perform at their best, and they prefer a mild climate.

▼ Succulents like this sempervivum are very wind-tolerant providing that they are planted in well-drained compost with plenty of gravel. The growing habit of these small, low-level plants protects them from strong winds.

◀ A mature purple phormium in a mild area makes a glorious pot-grown plant for an exposed roof terrace site. I like the way the grasses grow in amongst the gravel around a pot of purple *Verbena bonariensis*.

▶ Phormiums and *Betula jacquemontii* are really tough customers and grow happily on an exposed canalside terrace. Birch trees create an excellent screen to increase privacy and grow well in large planters. However, these deciduous trees shed their leaves in winter but the bare white stems will still look attractive.

are confined, there is more likelihood of the plant drying out due to the limited reserves of water. In addition plants in containers sit higher than those in beds, so are far more exposed.

The most open position is a roof garden where there is little protection offered by surrounding buildings. Try planting phormiums, pyracanthas, escallonias,

eucalyptus, rhamnus – all tough evergreens. In addition, bamboos like *Phyllostachys aurea* and *P. nigra* are tough though these can look scrappy in winter. In a large space use green phormiums to act as a filter and slow down the wind. I also rate some of the conifers like taxus, pines and picea. These are naturally hardy and their needle-like foliage is wind-resistant. Many plants that

grow near the sea are also useful, including cordyline, trachycarpus and tamarix.

Smaller plants are easier to find for an exposed site. Hebes are very wind-tolerant, the smaller-leafed ones tend to be hardiest, and olearias, spiraeas, yuccas, lavateras and genistas, are all good in these conditions. Many heathers and alpines and some of the ornamental grasses are also suitable.

METHOD

• Cover the existing drainage hole with a layer of crocks and fill with soil-based compost with a couple of scoops of horticultural grit mixed in to improve drainage and to help add weight to keep the pot stable.

• After flowering, cut back the euphorbia fronds. Feed sparingly with a balanced fertilizer.

• Do not allow the rhamnus to grow taller than 1m (3ft) – any more height and a strong wind might force the display over. Cut back the rhamnus in late spring to encourage bushy growth. Trim back long stems in late autumn at the end of the growing season.

wind-tolerant evergreens

This display provides an evergreen breath of fresh air, and the combination of plants, silvered terracotta and shells remind me of being close to the sea. It shows how matching the pot with the plants is important – the silvering of the terracotta surface is perfectly matched by the grey and variegated tones of the foliage. *Rhamnus alaternus* 'Argenteovariegata' is a lovely variegated evergreen that is wind-tolerant. In cold areas, the plain green-leafed form (*Rhamnus alaternus*) is hardier than the variegated form, or use a species of pyracanthus. *Euphorbia myrsinites* has tough succulent leaves which curl up attractively at the edge of the pot. Other options to create similar colour and texture to euphorbia include *Thymus* 'Silver Queen' or *Hebe pagei*.

PLANTING MATERIALS

Terracotta pot

Crocks

Horticultural grit

Soil-based compost

PLANTS

Euphorbia myrsinites

Rhamnus alaternus 'Argenteovariegata'

PLANT ALTERNATIVES

Hebe pagei

Pyracantha species

Thymus 'Silver Queen'

season

seasonal colour

Bedding plants and flowering bulbs can be used in containers to create purely seasonal displays and provide a rich burst of instant flower colour. Alternatively, they can be mixed in with permanent plantings to help extend the display's season and then lifted out when past their best.

Managing to keep pot-grown displays looking attractive for most of the year is part of the challenge of being a container gardener. The smaller the space the more important it is to make every pot look its best at all times as every detail will be noticed. But, simply plugging a gap as and when it appears, or even constant deadheading and pot maintenance is perhaps not the best solution.

Nowadays the choice of seasonal colour is vast, and many of these plants have been specially bred to grow well in containers. A display that has one star plant and space to add seasonal plant material can become an all-year-round performer. For example, a camellia shrub underplanted with polyanthus in early spring, busy lizzies in summer and cyclamen in autumn and winter really holds your interest throughout the year. Pansies

▶ In early summer, a group of table-top containers filled with flowering bedding plants like *Bellis perennis* and campanula can help to produce a dazzling display, which can be replaced later in the year for continuity of colour.

▶▶ Petunias planted in a deep pot can produce substantial mounds of flowers – far more dramatic than if grown in shallower soil. Feed regularly with a flowering food to encourage budding.

have also revolutionised the choice of flower colour available in winter. The colour range is expanding all the time. My own personal favourites are the burnt orange and copper-toned pansy flowers.

Containers planted with just one type of spring, summer or autumn bulb can also be a stunning way to add seasonal colour. I am a traditionalist and like to grow plants in their proper season. Seeing geraniums on sale in full flower in early March feels fundamentally wrong, particularly when there are plenty of glorious spring bulbs to add colour to your pots. A tub of spring tulips looks good not only for their flowers, but for the fresh green stalks which build one's expectation for the coming season. A shallow dish of jonquilla narcissi look delicate massed together, and summer lilies demand their own stage to perform at their beautiful best. If space is limited, plant seasonal bulbs in a plastic pot, and use the ornamental one as a "sleeve" so that the plants can be easily replaced once the flowering season is over. But bear in mind that the space between the plastic and ornamental pot is "slug heaven", so separate out the pots once in a while to pick off these hungry predators. Snowdrops fit into the winter bulb category but will also multiply quite happily if left undisturbed in a container. Because their foliage is small and discreet snowdrops do not have to be lifted once they have finished flowering but can continue growing amongst a permanent container planting.

For those gardeners who want low-maintenance container gardens, there are new varieties of geraniums that will drop their dead heads after they flower, though I happen to enjoy the simple repetition involved in this task. The range of fuchsias is huge, and some of the more subtle, elegant narrow flowers are exquisite for pot-grown displays. Petunias are often deliciously scented, and the trailing varieties such as the double *Petunia* Tumberlina Priscilla can fill a whole tub like a colourful mop of hair. More recent introductions like

Angelonia 'Angelface' are summer-flowering with fine blue or white petals. *Arctotis* (African daisy) make for a great display in themselves. I appreciate the combination of daisy-like apricot flowers and silver-green foliage. New forms of nemesia are delightful, trailing slightly with bi-coloured flowers. Try choosing varieties that are scented like *Nemesia* 'Karoo'. Bracteantha also have daisy flowerheads that continue flowering for six months, and again are a wonderful feature in themselves. The trailing verbenas, such as 'Sissinghurst' are superb, while the taller *Verbena bonariensis* with its flat heads of purple flowers is one of the finest of "interminglers" for a really large planter, and often comes through the winter unscathed. Other half-hardy plants, like penstemons, make both fine container plants and are excellent in borders.

One of my favourite flowers – the sweet pea – can grow successfully in large containers, and they look wonderful climbing up a trellis or wigwam structure. Also nasturtiums flower prolifically throughout summer and well into autumn.

Foliage plants, like coleus, are a welcome addition to the range of seasonal colour. In a mixed display, I think their beauty is lost so I prefer to use them on their own. A planter given the "coleus treatment" has real impact. Plants with both foliage and flower effects, like *Geranium* 'Midnight Reiter', which has intense purple foliage and lilac flowers, is also worthwhile.

I have already written about using perennials as seasonal colour, but I think it's worth reiterating that shrubs can be bought for container use when in flower and then transferred into the garden. I keep them in their plastic pot so that they can be lifted out again when required. Rhododendrons and azaleas can also be used in this way. They produce spectacular flowers for a short period. I then lift out the plants – with their plastic pot intact – and transfer them to a border. This frees up the container for the next seasonal star.

◀◀ I use the startling red of *Dahlia* 'Bishop of Llandaff' as seasonal late summer colour to create a bit of fire and passion in the border. This display shows harmony with the red foliage of coleus and *Lobelia cardinalis*.

◀◀ Cyclamen can bring months of autumn and winter cheer. The large-flowered forms are now bred to be more frost-resistant and less tender, with fine mottled leaves, and many have a sweet, subtle scent.

◀ I prefer to see hyacinths growing in containers rather than flower beds. Their upright habit seems to suit containers, and the pot height makes their delicious fragrance more accessible. Also, they can be lifted out once they have finished flowering.

◀ Tulips present an exquisite late spring show, not only because of their beautiful flowers but because they are a harbinger of summer. Protect tulip bulbs from hungry squirrels by placing a couple of spiky twigs just below the soil surface.

◀ Somehow an olive in the garden adds something magical, making it feel more special. Olive trees make fine evergreens which in a protected courtyard site can stay out all year. Placing container-grown trees in a border amongst established plants can add extra interest and height.

▶ *Nandina domestica* and *cryptomeria* are evergreens that give great displays for several months unlike the fleeting leaf colour of deciduous trees. These evergreen leaves turn a rust colour in late autumn and this stays all the way through the winter.

all-year-round colour

If chosen with care, some container plants can continue to look fantastic all year round rather than being limited to one season. A framework of these displayed in pots can help to create permanent interest and will mean that you do not need to go to the expense and effort of changing the display.

In any garden I love to witness the different seasons and to enjoy the natural changes that they bring. In a large garden, the whole area doesn't have to look spectacular in every season but in a small space it becomes more important to select plants that perform well throughout the year.

There are some plants that give shape and leaf-cover through the year. For example, box (*Buxus sempervirens*) will form an evergreen framework. One of the merits of box is that it is easy to clip into shape. It can be sculpted into a ball or pyramid, or cut into a simple square. A piece of "living architecture" made out of box helps to unite the house and hard surfaces within the garden, and looks powerful whatever the season. Other evergreens that clip well are privet, holly and yew, though it is worth experimenting with others.

There are plants that naturally grow into architectural or even sculptural shapes without the need for clipping. *Cupressus sempervirens* 'Stricta', the Italian cypress, stands tall presenting a dark outline against the sky. Conversely, the slightly amorphous mound of a *Genista lydia* will tumble out of a container, creating an attractive, informal shape and then will suddenly light up with bright yellow, pea-like flowers in spring. The architectural silhouette of *Mahonia* 'Charity' is also striking and combines panicles of scented yellow flowers in winter with serrated evergreen leaves.

▶ *Pittosporum* 'Garnettii' is one of the finest of variegated evergreens – their leaves developing an attractive pink tinge in the cold of winter. At that time, I move this display closer to the house so that it is in full view. Being able to shift containers around from one place to another means that you can alter the appearance of the garden throughout the year with the minimum of fuss.

▼ The cabbage-like leaves of *Bergenia cordifolia* create a ruffle of decorative leaves at the neck of this concrete container while red cordyline leaves fan out like tail feathers. In winter, the bergenia leaves will also turn red and then the plant will flower in spring. The pansies are a winter addition to an otherwise all-year-round display.

Plenty of container-grown evergreens can look good all year round. One of my favourite, *Pittosporum* 'Tom Thumb' is a dwarf form with dark purple foliage, and looks at home in most styles of container. Sarcococca is an extremely hardy, shade-tolerant evergreen with tiny white-scented flowers in winter. Another worthy evergreen which has good all-year-round merits is *Choisya ternata*. The soft green foliage makes a good foil for other plants, it flowers once in spring and then often has a second flush in late summer. Added to that, the foliage releases a fragrant orangey aroma. The golden forms *Choisya ternata* 'Sundance' and 'Goldfinger' also grow particularly well in containers. *Arbutus unedo*, the strawberry tree, has good flowers, berries and neat evergreen foliage. The smaller growing ceanothus are valuable, and 'Yankee Point' has the best habit for a container because it grows to about 1.2m (4ft).

Bamboos and evergreen grasses are of interest because of their all-year-round colour, and for their gentle, swaying movement. The lovely blue-grey leaves of *Helictotrichon sempervirens* are topped with masses of slender flowers that wave gracefully in the breeze. I also rather like the shaggy mane of *Carex* 'Evergold' which always appears ebullient and cheerful.

Less obvious all-year-round interest can be provided by quite surprising plants. Part of my passion for agapanthus is that I like the look of the evergreen species in winter which have floppy strap-shaped leaves, as well as the wonderful flowers and seedheads in summer and autumn. Purple sage can look slightly sulky in winter, but sage leaves covered in frost is an attractive sight. *Hydrangea petiolaris* in a pot looks stark in winter, but has fascinating bark. *Rhododendron yakushumanum* has gorgeous pink buds and spectacular white flowers. I grow it for its dark olive-green foliage and its compact form that always looks good in a container. Olive trees themselves make wonderful pot-grown evergreens, provided the leaves are protected from severe frosts.

Tree and shrub bark can be fascinating throughout the year. For example, the stunning bark of ericaceous *Stuartia sinensis*, together with the many different birch trees, and maples. One of the best plants to combine autumn colour with other season's interest is the peeling bark maple, *Acer griseum*. Also, the polished peeling bark of *Prunus serrula* is worth considering as the bark glows in winter, and this species will grow well in a large planter.

Autumn colours are more fleeting and a less predictable attribute of a plant. In a windy site, I have watched maple leaves colouring up one day and shedding their leaves the next. The evergreens nandina and cryptomeria, however, will provide lovely autumn effects that continue into winter. Autumn also heralds the arrival of colourful berries. Pyracantha, skimmia and cotoneasters are all useful evergreens with handsome berries.

Covering walls with evergreen or semi-evergreen climbers (keeping its leaves in mild winters, or when sheltered by a wall) is often a useful way of greening up a hard surface. *Akebia quinata* is a fascinating evergreen with weird purple flowers which appear in late winter and are delicately scented. The huge range of ivy is also well worth considering for their all-year-round coverage, leaf shape and colour. Trachelospermum is one of the finest of evergreen climbers, because of its glossy leaves and sweetly scented white flowers that continue throughout the summer. It seems to thrive when its roots are contained which makes it well-suited to container gardening. *Solanum jasminoides* is a semi-evergreen which needs a large container because it grows so fast. It produces flowers that go on all through the summer and into the autumn. I would also recommend *Clematis cirrhosa* for its glossy slightly serrated foliage and delicate almost translucent primrose-yellow flowers in winter.

▼ *Trachelospermum jasminoides* must be one of the finest of evergreen climbers for a container. It has fragrant white flowers all summer, and dark, glossy foliage all year round which makes a good screen. It is slow-growing but you can buy mature plants for instant impact.

care

potting-up

The way that you prepare a container will make all the difference to how well the plants grow. Provide five-star treatment which includes a clean container interior, good drainage, fresh compost and healthy plants and you will be rewarded.

When buying plants, look for bushy specimens that have not been forced to grow on quickly in greenhouse conditions. Early season sweet basil that has been forced, for example, gets such a shock when it is put outside that it usually keels over and dies. You can recognise forced plants as they always look slightly too glossy and often appear to be flowering earlier than they should.

With fast-growing species, I plant them directly into large containers (even though they look a bit lost for a while) as re-potting large climbers and trees from a medium-sized pot to a slightly larger one is quite difficult to achieve without damaging the plant. Most

1 Plenty of gravel and crocks at the bottom of the pot help to ensure good drainage, and prevent the plant roots from becoming waterlogged. With large containers, use pieces of polystyrene instead, to reduce the final weight of the planted-up container.

2 Carefully lower the plant into the pot, supporting it with two hands around the root ball rather than holding the stem. Fill in around the plant with compost until it sits about 2.5cm (1in) below the rim. With a single specimen, take care to centre and straighten it.

3 A mulch of gravel on the surface will help conserve moisture by limiting evaporation from the compost. It will also prevent weeds from growing. Ornamental mulches (*see Care: Mulching*) can do the job just as well, though gravel has a really horticultural feel.

container-grown plants prefer their roots to be quite restricted, so choose a container not much bigger than the plastic pot you have bought it in. Once you have selected your container make sure that it has adequate drainage holes and put in a layer of crocks or gravel at the bottom. Choose a suitable soil mix for the species, for example lime-haters such as camellias require an ericaceous compost. Soil-based compost is heavier, holds nutrients better, and is more appropriate for permanent plantings, while multi-purpose compost is lighter, and good for seasonal displays. With most plants I prefer to use an equal mix of soil-based compost and peat-free multi-purpose compost and a scoop of horticultural grit to improve drainage. With Mediterranean plants and others that really appreciate well-drained soil use more grit in the mix. This will help protect the plants from waterlogging and freezing in winter.

If the root ball of the plant is really tight and compact when you lift it out of its pot before planting, tease out the roots slightly, so that they can start to spread out quickly and gain a foothold in the fresh soil. Plant so that the level of the soil is about 2.5cm (1in) below the rim of the pot. Once in the container, it is essential to water the plants in well, and then water them again. Freshly planted specimens need a thorough drenching.

Plants that have been growing in a container for several years may need to be re-potted to maintain their health and vigour, even if you have been top dressing and feeding the plants. Choose a new container slightly larger than the existing one. Then lift the plants and brush some of the old soil out of the root ball. To anchor the plants, gently pour in fresh compost around the sides, and press it down gently with your hand until the container is full to the rim. Move the pot to your intended location and then water well. Add more compost after watering, if necessary, and mulch the surface.

1 Use a power drill to make a series of evenly spaced holes in the base of a wooden window box. This will ensure adequate drainage for the plant roots. It is a common mistake to have too few holes which can easily get blocked up even if a layer of gravel has been added.

2 Before filling with compost, place a generous layer of gravel in the bottom of the container, particularly if you are planting herbs, alpines or Mediterranean plants as they will grow best in well-drained soil.

mulching

Mulching is the icing on the cake, only easier. Nothing in the preparation of a container is so simple, quick and rewarding. Mulches look good, they help the container to conserve moisture, suppress weed growth, and provide a slight barrier against slug and snail attack. I like to consider the other hard surfaces present in the garden before I choose a suitable mulching material for containers. In my garden there are cockle shells on one flower bed, gravel on the path and a slate-covered raised bed. I use these same materials as mulch in planters to help integrate them with the garden. Mulches can also help to create a story or picture: cockle shells become part of a seaside theme; bark chippings a woodland, and shiny pieces of broken-up compact discs give a modern edge. Take care though, too many quirky mulches will distract from the containers and their plantings.

When mulching, always make sure that the compost is wet before applying the mulch and then the mulch will lock this moisture in. I remove the mulch every couple of years to top dress the container (*see Care: Watering and Feeding page 137*) and then either wash the mulch and put it back or use a new material. Changing the mulch can help to subtly change the appearance of your container without changing the plants. When a planting has matured in a container, (particularly a plant with a bushy habit) it fills the pot, and prevents weed growth and evaporation without the need for a mulch.

1 One of my favourite mulches is broken pieces of slate. This natural material is austere and works well in modern stone planters.

2 Cockle shells used as mulch help to create a seaside atmosphere.

3 Dyed broken shells are fun for individual displays, particularly if the colour coordinates with the plants and planter. Many different shell colours are available.

4 Cobble stones are a heavy-duty mulch. I delight in rearranging cobbles which shows how much pleasure can be found in very ordinary gardening tasks!

5 Iron shavings are one of the more bizarre by-products that are now used as mulch. In time, this metal loses its sheen which creates a rather lovely changing effect.

6 Dyed crushed safety glass from car window screens make an excellent mulch with no sharp edges. The effect is contemporary and works with thin-stemmed plants like bamboo where a lot of the top surface of the container is on view.

7 Carefully chosen mulches can be worked in between plants with low-growing habits. Here, pink stones cover ground between succulents and create an interesting layer of pattern and texture.

watering and feeding

Watering is an essential routine required to care for plants grown in containers. You can forget to feed the plant for a season and they may get a little starved but they won't die. You can skip pruning for a year or two and you may get a slightly oversized specimen, but forget to water the plants for a week in a dry, hot summer and you can suffer severe damage and, at worst, the plants can end up dead. Some plants are more tolerant of drought and can survive for far longer periods between watering. My own yuccas and agaves seem to thrive pretty well when watered only sporadically. But thirsty plants like pelargoniums, geraniums, even lavenders can quickly start to suffer from lack of water. But don't just assume that a plant with dried-out leaves is dead. One of my lavenders looked beyond saving but after a thorough watering, it quickly recovered.

Watering containers is a matter of routine. During hot sunny spells check pots every day, and try and water the plants in the cool of the morning or evening to prevent the leaves from becoming scorched. Water thoroughly into the roots. Don't assume that just because the top soil looks damp that the pot is well watered.

During hot spells, I like to give my container-grown plants plenty of water and I try not to always water the pot from the same side, even if access is difficult. When compost (particularly coir-based ones) get too dry it can be difficult to rehydrate them. Containers that have dried out need a real drenching, or better still sink them into a bucket of water and let them soak up the liquid.

When I go on holiday, I move containers into a sheltered, shady area, so that they are less susceptible to drying out. Setting up a simple irrigation system can save a lot of trouble, and there are good-value systems available at garden centres that can be programmed to drip or spray water into the container at regular intervals. Because I move my pots about quite often, I prefer to water by hand but irrigation systems are useful when going away.

Overwatering can be just as much of a problem for plants as lack of water, especially during the winter when the plants are dormant. If the plant is not growing and water is not evaporating, a waterlogged soil can drown the roots depriving them of oxygen.

Feed foliage plants and leafy edibles with a fertilizer high in nitrogen, and feed flowering and fruiting plants with a tomato feed or one high in potassium to encourage as many flowers and fruit as possible. Trees and shrubs will flourish if given a top-dressing of bonemeal in autumn to strengthen the root system. In a well-established pot, I top-dress the soil with a layer of well-rotted manure every two years to add nutrients to the soil in the pot, or I scrape off the top 2.5cm (1in) of soil and add fresh compost to give the mature planting a boost.

◀ Basic watering aids like a plastic bottle cut in half act as a mini-reservoir for water, and help to ensure that the water penetrates down into the deeper root system of the plant.

▶ An irrigation system can be programmed to switch on and off at regular intervals, ensuring that watering takes place even when you are away. The water drip-feeders are staked into the soil and have to be lifted out and checked from time to time to make sure that the water pipe has not become blocked up with limescale.

◀ Pick off the dead pansy flowerheads regularly to encourage new flowers. That way the energy that the plants would have put into seed production goes back into budding and flowering. Old flowerheads are also removed for aesthetic reasons so that they don't spoil the beauty of the plant in full flower.

▶ Trimming box topiary by hand with garden shears is both a relaxing and rewarding task. When cutting large-leaved topiary plants like bay (*Laurus nobilis*), cut the stems rather than the leaves. Stand back from time to time to check the shape.

pruning

Trimming pot-grown plants at least once a year has several advantages. It will help keep the plants in proportion to the pot, keep the plants healthy and increase flower and foliage production. Timing is important because cutting back plants at the wrong time can remove the flowering wood and produce leafy growth instead. Plants that flower early in the season, such as flowering quince, flower on old wood, and are best cut back after flowering. Late flowerers, such as caryopteris, flower on this season's growth and should be cut back early in the season. Mediterranean plants appreciate being trimmed back after flowering to stop them becoming too leggy.

Cutting back also helps create bushier specimens. A bushier plant in a container not only looks better but helps to avoid instability – wind tends to catch tall, thin specimens.

Many of the evergreens simply need a light trim to tidy up their appearance but if you are trying to create a topiary shape they will need more attention. I find myself clipping my box plants quite regularly, because it is so relaxing nipping out new growth between my fingers. The slower-growing specimens like yew may only need a trim twice a year – once in spring and once in autumn.

Dead-heading helps to keep plants looking their best. For example, geraniums look far better with their old flowerheads and stalks picked off. Dead-heading some plants, like violas, helps to ensure that the energy of the plant goes into producing more flowers. It's also worth trimming back vigorous seasonal plants if they are taking over a display. Plants like argyranthemum will soon recover and flower again and pelargoniums can produce a second flush of flowers if cut back once the first flush is over.

the author's shop in London

Planters East
82 Columbia Road, London E2 7RG
Tel: 020 7739 3336
www.planterseast.com
Planted-up containers, pots and plants and a range of consultancy services.

specialist containers

Architectural plants
Cooks Farm, Nuthurst, Horsham,
West Sussex, RH13 6LH
Email: Architecturalplants@horsham.intelynx.net
Tel: 01403 642130
Specialists in unusual plants.

Gardens and Beyond
47 Highgate High Street, London, N6 5JX
Tel: 020 8340 3409
www.gardensbeyond.com
Contemporary planters and design service.

Graham Greener
27 Harbour Street, Whitstable, Kent, CT5 1AH
Tel: 01227 277100
www.grahamgreener.com
New and old containers.

Mark Pedro de la Torre
The Court Yard, The Old Rectory, Stoke Lacy,
Hereford, HR7 4HH
Email: delatorre@lineone.net
Tel: 01432 820500
Unusual terracotta planters.

The Plant Room
47 Barnsbury Street, London, N1 1TP
Tel: 020 7700 6766
www.plantroom.co.uk
Contemporary planters and design service.

Pots and Pithoi
The Barns, East Street, Turners Hill,
West Sussex, RH10 4QQ
Tel: 01342 714793
www.potsandpithoi.com
Imported containers from Crete.

The Red Mud Hut
92 Columbia Road
London E2 7QB
Tel: 020 7613 4811
Fantastic range of containers from all round the world.

Woodhams Flower and Garden Store
45 Elizabeth Street, Belgravia, London, SW1W 9PP
Tel: 020 7730 3353
www.woodhams.co.uk
Contemporary planters and garden design service.

recommended garden centres

Armitage's Mower World & Garden Centre
75 Birchencliffe Hill Road, Huddersfield,
West Yorkshire, HD3 3NJ
Tel: 01484 536010
Email: enquiries@armitages.uk.com
www.armitages.uk.com

Aylett Nurseries Ltd
North Orbital Road, St. Albans,
Hertfordshire, AL2 1DH
Tel: 01727 822255
Email: enquiries@armitages.uk.com
www.armitages.uk.com

Barton Grange Garden Centre
Chester Road, Woodford, Cheshire, SK7 1QS
Tel: 0161 439 0745
www.bartongrange.co.uk

Bents Garden Centre & Nurseries
Warrington Road, Glazebury, Leigh End,
Nr Warrington, Cheshire, WA3 5NT
Tel: 01942 266300
Email: info@bents.fsnet.co.uk
www.bents.co.uk

Camden Garden Centre
2 Barkers Drive, St. Pancras Way, London, NW1 0JW
Tel: 020 7387 7080
www.camdengardencentre.co.uk

Capital Gardens
1 Townsend Yard, Highgate, London, N6 5JP
Tel: 020 8348 5054
www.capitalgardens.co.uk

Clifton Nurseries
5a Clifton Villas, Maida Vale, London, W9 2PH
Tel: 020 7289 6851
www.clifton.co.uk

Coolings Nurseries
Rushmore Hill, Knockholt, Nr Sevenoaks,
Kent, TN14 7NN
Tel: 01959 532269
www.coolings.co.uk

Dobbies Garden Centres Plc
Dobbies Garden World
Lasswade, Midlothian, EH18 1AZ
Tel: 0131 663 1941
www.dobbies.com

Forest Lodge Garden Centre
Holt Pound, Farnham, Surrey, GU10 4LD
Tel: 01420 23275
Email: sales@forest-lodge.co.uk
www.forest-lodge.co.uk

Frosts Garden Centre
Newport Road, Woburn Sands, Milton Keynes
Buckinghamshire, MK17 8UE
Tel: 01908 583511
www.frostsgroup.com

Haskins Garden Centre
Longham, Ferndown, Dorset, BH22 9DG
Tel: 01202 591919
www.haskins.co.uk

Mid-Ulster Garden Centre
35 Station Road, Maghera,
County Londonderry, BT46 5BS
Tel: 028 796 42324
www.midulster.co.uk

Squires Garden Centre
Sixth Cross Road, Twickenham
Middlesex, TW2 5PA
Tel: 0208 9779241/2/3
www.squiresgardencentres.co.uk.

Stewarts Garden-Lands
Lyndhurst Road, Somerford, Christchurch,
Dorset, BH23 4SA
Tel: 01425 272244
www.stewarts.co.uk

Thurrock Garden Centre
South Road, South Ockendon, Essex, RM15 6DU
Tel: 01708 851991
Email: info@thurrockgardencentre.co.uk
www.thurrockgardencentre.co.uk

Trelawney Garden Leisure
Sladesbridge, Wadebridge, Cornwall, PL27 6JA
Tel: 01208 812966
Email: enquiries@trelawney.co.uk
www.trelawney.co.uk

The Van Hage Garden Company
Great Amwell, Ware, Hertfordshire, SG12 9RP
Tel: 01920 870811
www.vanhage.co.uk

Webbs of Wychbold
Wychbold, Droitwich Spa, Worcestershire, WR9 0DG
Tel: 01527 860000
Email: info@webbsofwychbold.co.uk
www.webbsofwychbold.co.uk

The Wisley Plant Centre
The RHS Garden, Wisley, Woking,
Surrey, GU23 6QB
Tel: 01483 211113
www.rhs.org.uk

Woodlands Nurseries
Ashby Road, Stapleton, Leicestershire, LE9 8JE
Tel: 01455 291494
Email: alan@woodlandsnurseries.freeserve.co.uk
www.woodlandsnurseries.co.uk

index

Page numbers in *italic*
refer to the illustrations

photographic credits

All photographs by Marianne Majerus but we would like to thank the following garden designers and locations for their help:

2-3 Mark Pedro de la Torre : 4-5 Inger Laan : 7 Joe Swift: 8 The Old Vicarage, East Ruston, Norfolk : 9 Old Vicarage Hill: 10 Mark Reeder : 11 Ruth Collier: 12-13 Michèle Osborne : 14 Gardens & Beyond: 15 Catharina Malmberg-Snodgrass:16 Bedfield Hall: 17 Joe Swift: 19 top Bruce Fursman: 20 Gardens & Beyond : 22 Mrs Ward : 23 Declan Buckley: 24 top left Terence Conran, RHS Chelsea 1999 : 24 top right David Viall: 25 Diana Yakeley: 26 John Watkins: 28 RHS Rosemoor: 29 Carole Vincent, Blue Circle Garden, RHS Chelsea 2001: 30 Schwebsange, Luxembourg: 31 Mark Pedro de la Torre : 35 Ruth Collier: 36-37 Mark Pedro de la Torre: 38-39 Coworth Garden Design: 40 RHS Wisley : 41 Declan Buckley: 42 Chris Marchant: 43 top David Viall: 43 bottom Pots & Pithoi: 46-47 David Viall: 48-49 Pots & Pithoi: 50 RHS Wisley: 52-53 Bourton House: 53 bottom 'Gardening Which', RHS Chelsea 2002 : 60 bottom right Michèle Osborne: 61 Carole Vincent, Blue Circle Garden, RHS Chelsea 2001: 64 inset Diana Yakeley: 64-65 The Flying Garden, design: Paul Cooper, RHS Chelsea 2000 : 66 Ward & Ben: 67 Nicole Albert with Gardens & Beyond: 68-69 Christopher Masson & Ian St John: 70 top and bottom Windy Hall: 71 Chelsea Flower Show, design: Stephen Woodhams: 72 Kim Whatmore: 73 top George Carter: 73 bottom Michael Clark and Simon Steele: 75 Joe Swift: 78 Adam Caplin: 78-79 Adam Caplin: 80 Stephanie Donaldson: 85 Simon Denman: 88 Ann-Marie Powell: 94-95 Paul Southern: 96 inset Stephen Anderton: 96-97 Christopher Masson: 98 right Stabredimus: 98 Adrian Gunning: 99 Lara Copley-Smith: 100-101 Ruth Collier: 106-107 Glen Chantry: 113 top Adam Caplin: 113 bottom Adam Caplin: 114 Declan Buckley: 115 right Michael Clark and Simon Steele: 115 left Joan Clifton (supplier: Avant Garden): 116 Gardens & Beyond: 117 Declan Buckley: 120-121 Bourton House, Glos: 125 bottom Malvern Terrace, London: 129 Gardens & Beyond: 130-131 Joe Swift: 134-135 Paul Southern: 134 centre right Anthony Collett 135 top 'Gardening Which', RHS Chelsea 2002: 144 Christopher Masson & Ian St John: endpapers The Chelsea Gardener.

author's acknowledgements

I would like to thank Marianne Majerus for her inspirational photographs, Bella Pringle for her clarity, patience and guidance and Maggie Town and Beverly Price for their wonderful design work.

Thanks to all at the Plant Room, Camden Garden Centre, Clifton Nurseries and Highgate Garden Centre, Priscilla Amos, Mervyn Reynolds and the team at Bypass Nurseries, Stuart Lowen at Ball Colegrave Ltd, Jim at Ball Seeds, Paula Pryke, Carolyn Hutchinson, Michael Clark, Lorna Harvey and a special big thank you to Lynne and Martin at the Red Mud Hut.

Thanks to all the many people whose gardens were photographed.